The Church Universal

Volume III

THE CHURCH AND THE BARBARIANS

THE CHURCH UNIVERSAL

BRIEF HISTORIES
OF HER CONTINUOUS LIFE

Edited by

THE REV. W. H. HUTTON, B.D.

FELLOW AND TUTOR OF S. JOHN'S COLLEGE, OXFORD,
EXAMINING CHAPLAIN TO THE BISHOP OF ROCHESTER

A SERIES of eight volumes dealing with the history of the Christian Church from the beginning to the present day, undertaken by contributors specially competent to deal with the periods on which they will write. Each volume will be complete in itself, but will be definitely related to the other volumes in the series. It is intended to deal clearly and succinctly with the outward history of the Church, and to include some accounts of the influence of individual churchmen and of great movements of thought and of devotion which have profoundly affected her life.

The volumes, now in course of publication, will be arranged as follows :—

LONDON: RIVINGTONS

THE CHURCH

AND THE BARBARIANS

BEING AN OUTLINE OF
THE HISTORY OF THE CHURCH
FROM A.D. 461 TO A.D. 1003

BY THE REV.

WILLIAM HOLDEN HUTTON, B.D.

FELLOW AND TUTOR OF S. JOHN BAPTIST COLLEGE, OXFORD
EXAMINING CHAPLAIN TO THE BISHOP OF ROCHESTER

NEW YORK
THE MACMILLAN COMPANY
1906

EDITORIAL NOTE

WHILE there is a general agreement among the writers as to principles, the greatest freedom as to treatment is allowed to writers in this series. The volumes, for example, will not be of the same length. Volume II., which deals with the formative period of the Church, is, not unnaturally, longer in proportion than the others. To Volume VI., which deals with the Reformation, will be allotted a similar extension. The authors, again, use their own discretion in such matters as footnotes and lists of authorities. But the aim of the series, which each writer sets before him, is to tell, clearly and accurately, the story of the Church, as a divine institution with a continuous life.

W. H. HUTTON

PREFACE

IT has seemed to me impossible to deal with the long period covered by this volume as briefly as the scheme of the series required without leaving out a great many events and concentrating attention chiefly upon a few central facts and a few important personages. I think that the main results of the development may thus be seen, though there is much which is here omitted that would have been included had the book been written on other lines.

Some pages find place here which originally appeared in *The Guardian* and *The Treasury*, and a few lines which once formed part of an article in *The Church Quarterly Review*. My thanks are due for the courtesy of the Editors. I have reprinted some passages from my *Church of the Sixth Century*, a book which is now out of print and not likely to be reissued.

I have to thank the Rev. L. Pullan for help from his wide knowledge, and Mr. L. Strachan, of Heidelberg, of whose accuracy and learning I have had long experience, for reading the proofs and making the index.

W. H. H.

S. John's College, Oxford,
Septuagesima, 1906.

CONTENTS

THE CHURCH
AND THE BARBARIANS

CHAPTER I

THE CHURCH AND ITS PROSPECTS
IN THE FIFTH CENTURY

THE year 461 saw the great organisation which had
ruled and united Europe for so long trembling into
decay. The history of the Empire in relation   The task
to Christianity is indeed a remarkable one.   of the
The imperial religion had been the neces-   Church.
sary and deadly foe of the religion of Jesus Christ : it
had fought and had been conquered. Gradually the
Empire itself with all its institutions and laws had been
transformed, at least outwardly, into a Christian power.
Questions of Christian theology had become questions
of imperial politics. A Roman of the second century
would have wondered indeed at the transformation
which had come over the world he knew: it seemed as
if the kingdoms of the earth had become the kingdoms
of the Lord and of His Christ. But also it seemed that
the new wine had burst the old bottles. The boundaries
of the Roman world had been outstepped : nations
had come in from the East and from the West. The

B

system which had been supreme was not elastic : the new ideas, Christian and barbarian alike, pressed upon it till it gave way and collapsed.   And so it came about that if Christianity had conquered the old world, it had still to conquer the new.

Now before the Church in the fifth century there were set several powers, interests, duties, with which
The decaying Empire. she was called upon to deal ; and her dealing with them was the work of the next five centuries.   They were,—the Empire, Christian but obsolescent; the new nations, still heathen, which were struggling for territory within the bounds of the Empire, and for sway over the imperial institutions ; the distant tribes untouched by the message of Christ; and the growth, within the Church itself, of new and great organisations, which were destined in great measure to guide and direct her work.   Politics, theology, organisation, missions, had all their share in the work of the Church from 461 to 1003.   In each we shall find her influence : to harmonise them we must find a principle which runs through her relation to them all.

The central idea of the period with which we are to deal is unity.   Up till the fifth century, till the Council of Chalcedon (451) completed the primary
The need of unity. definition of the orthodox Christian faith in the person of the Lord Jesus Christ, Christians were striving for conversion, organisation, definition.   All these aims still remained, but in less prominence.   The Church's order was completed, the Church's creed was practically fixed, and the dominant nations in Europe had owned the name of Christ. There remained a new and severe test.   Would the

Church win the new barbarian conquerors as she had won the old imperial power ? There was to be a great epoch of missionary energy. But of the firm solidity of the Church there could be no doubt. Heresies had torn from her side tribes and even nations who had once belonged to her fold. But still unity was triumphant in idea; 'and it was into the Catholic unity of the visible Church that the new nations were to be invited to enter. S. Augustine's grand idea of the City of God had really triumphed, before the fifth century was half passed, over the heathen conceptions of political rule. The Church, in spite of the tendency to separate already visible in East and West, was truly one; and that unity was represented also in the Christian Empire. "At the end of the fifth century the only Christian countries outside the limits of the Empire were Ireland and Armenia, and Armenia, maintaining a precarious existence beside the great Persian monarchy of the Sassanid kings, had been for a long time virtually dependent on the Roman power." [1] Politically, while tyrants rise and fall, and barbarian hosts, the continuance of the Wandering of the Nations, sweep across the stage, we are struck above all by the significant fact which Mr. Freeman (*Western Europe in the Fifth Century*) knew so well how to make emphatic:—"The wonderful thing is how often the Empire came together again. What strikes us at every step in the tangled history of these times is the wonderful life which the Roman name and the Roman Power still kept when it was thus attacked on every side from without and torn in pieces in every quarter from within." And the reason for this indubitably was that the

[1] Bryce, *Holy Roman Empire*, p. 13, ed. 1904.

Empire had now another organisation to support it, based on the same idea of central unity. One Church stood beside one Empire, and became year by year even more certain, more perfect, as well as more strong. In the West the papal power rose as the imperial decayed, and before long came near to replacing it. In the East, where the name and tradition of old Rome was always preserved in the imperial government, the Church remained in that immemorial steadfastness to the orthodox faith which was a bond of unity such as no other idea could possibly supply. In the educational work which the emperors had to undertake in regard to the tribes which one by one accepted their sway, the Christian Church was their greatest support. In East as well as West, the bishops, saints, and missionaries were the true leaders of the nations into the unity of the Empire as well as the unity of **The Church's conquest of barbarism.** the Church. The idea of Christian unity saved the Empire and taught the nations. The idea of Christian unity was the force which conquered barbarism and made the barbarians children of the Catholic Church and fellow-citizens with the inheritors of the Roman traditions.

If the dominant idea of the long period with which this book is to deal is the unity of the Church, seen through the struggles to preserve, to teach, or to attain it, the most important facts are those which belong to the conversion, to Christ and to the full faith of the Catholic Church, of races new to the Western world. The gradual extinction in Italy of the Goths, the conversion of the Franks, of the English, of many races on distant barbarian borderlands of civilisation, the acceptance of Catholicism by the Lombards and

the Western Goths, do not complete the historical
tale, though they are a large part of it: there was the
falling back in Africa and for a long time in Europe of
the settlements of the Cross before the armies of the
Crescent. There were also two other important
features of this long-extended age, to which writers
have given the name of dark. There was the survival
of ancient learning, which lived on through the flood of
barbarian immigration into the lands which had been
its old home, yet was very largely eclipsed by the predominance of theological interests in literature. And
there was the growth of a strong ecclesiastical power,
based upon an orthodox faith (though not without
hesitations and lapses), and gradually winning a
formidable political dominion. That power was the
Roman Papacy.

CHAPTER II

THE EMPIRE AND THE EASTERN CHURCH
(461–628)

WHEN the death of Leo the Great in 461 removed from the world of religious progress a saintly and dominant figure whose words were listened to in East and West as were those of no other man of his day, the interest of Church history is seen to turn decisively to the East.

The story of Eastern Christendom is unique. There is the fascinating tale of the union of Greek meta-

Character of the Greek Church. physics and Christian theology, and its results, so fertile, so vigorous, so intensely interesting as logical processes, so critical as problems of thought. For the historian there is a story of almost unmatched attraction ; the story of how a people was kept together in power, in decay, in failure, in persecution, by the unifying force of a Creed and a Church. And there is the extraordinary missionary development traceable all through the history of Eastern Christianity : the wonderful Nestorian missions, the activity of the evangelists, imperial and hierarchical, of the sixth century, the conversion of Russia, the preludes to the remarkable achievements in modern times of orthodox missions in the Far East.

Throughout the whole of the long period indeed

which begins with the death of Leo and ends with that
of Silvester II., though the Latin Church was growing
in power and in missionary success, it was probably the
Christianity of the East which was the most secure and
the most prominent. Something of its work may well
be told at the beginning of our task.

The last years of the fifth century were in the main
occupied in the East by the dying down of a controversy which had rent the Church. The   The
Eutychian heresy, condemned at Chalcedon,   Monophy-
gave birth to the Monophysite party, which   site
spread widely over the East. Attempts   contro-
were soon made to bridge over the gulf by   versy.
taking from the decisions of Chalcedon all that definitely repudiated the Monophysite opinions. In 482
the patriarch Acacius of Constantinople, under the
orders probably of the Emperor Zeno (474–91), drew
up the *Henotikon*, an endeavour to secure
the peace of the Church by abandoning the   The
definitions of the Fourth General Council.   Henotikon.
No longer was "one and the same Christ, Son, Lord,
only-begotten, acknowledged *in two natures*, without
fusion, without change, without division, without
separation." But it is impossible to ignore a controversy which has been a cause of wide divergence.
Men will not be silent, or forget, when they are told.
Statesmanlike was, no doubt, the policy which sought
for unity by ignoring differences; and peace was to
some extent secured in the East so long as Zeno and
his successor Anastasius (491–518) reigned. But at
Rome it was not accepted. Such a document, which
implicitly repudiated the language of Leo the Great,
which the Fourth General Council had adopted, could

never be accepted by the whole Church; and those in
the East who were theologians and philosophers rather
than statesmen saw that the question once raised
must be finally settled in the dogmatic decisions of the
Church. Had the Lord two Natures, the Divine
and Human, or but one? The reality of the Lord's
Humanity as well as of His Divinity was a truth
which, at whatever cost of division and separation, it
was essential that the Church should proclaim and
cherish.

In Constantinople, a city always keen to debate
theology in the streets, the divergence was plainly
manifest; and a document which was "subtle to escape
subtleties" was not likely to be satisfactory to the
subtlest of controversialists. The Henotikon was accepted at Antioch, Jerusalem, and Alexandria, but it
was rejected by Rome and by the real sense of Constantinople. In Alexandria the question was only laid
for a time, and when a bishop who had been elected
was refused recognition by Acacius the Patriarch of
Constantinople and Peter "the Stammerer," who accepted the Henotikon, preferred to his place, a reference to Rome led to a peremptory letter from Pope
Simplicius, to which Acacius paid no heed whatever.
Felix II. (483–92), after an ineffectual embassy, actu-
ally declared Acacius excommunicate and deposed.
The monastery of the Akoimetai at Constantinople
("sleepless ones," who kept up perpetual intercession)
threw itself strongly on to the side of the advocates of
Chalcedon. Acacius, then excommunicated by Rome
because he would not excommunicate the Monophysite
patriarch of Alexandria, retorted by striking out the
name of Felix from the diptychs of the Church.

It was the first formal beginning of the schism
which,—temporarily, and again and again, healed,—was
ultimately to separate East and West; and
it was due, as so many misfortunes of the
Church have been, to the inevitable divergence between those who thought of theology
first as statesmen and those who thought first as in-
quirers after the truth. The schism spread more
widely. In Syria Monophysitism joined Nestorianism
in the confusion of thought: in Egypt the Coptic
Church arose which repudiated Chalcedon: Abyssinia
and Southern India were to follow. Arianism had in
the East practically died away; Nestorianism was
powerful only in far-away lands, but Monophysitism
was for a great part of the sixth century strong in the
present, and close to the centre of Church life. The
sixth century began, as the fifth had ended, in strife
from which there seemed no outway. Nationalism, and
the rival claims of Rome and Constantinople, complicated the issues.

Under Anastasius, the convinced opponent of the
Council of Chalcedon and himself to all intents a
Monophysite in opinion, some slight negotiations were
begun with Rome, while the streets of Constantinople
ran with blood poured out by the hot advocates of
theological dogma. In 515 legates from Pope Hormisdas visited Constantinople; in 516 the emperor sent
envoys to Rome; in 517 Hormisdas replied, not only
insisting on the condemnation of those who had
opposed Chalcedon, but also claiming from the Cæsar
the obedience of a spiritual son; and in that same year
Anastasius, "most sweet-tempered of emperors," died,
rejecting the papal demands.

> Schism
> between
> East and
> West.

The accession of Justin I. (518–27) was a triumph
for the orthodox faith, to which the people of Constantinople had firmly held. The patriarch, John the
Cappadocian, declared his adherence to the Fourth
Council: the name of Pope Leo was put on the
diptychs together with that of S. Cyril; and synod
after synod acclaimed the orthodox faith. Negotiations for reunion with the West were immediately
opened. The patriarch and the emperor wrote to
Pope Hormisdas, and there wrote also a theologian
more learned than the patriarch, the Emperor's
nephew, Justinian. "As soon," he wrote, "as the
Emperor had received by the will of God the princely
fillet, he gave the bishops to understand that the peace
of the Church must be restored. This had already in
a great degree been accomplished." But the pope's
opinion must be taken with regard to the condemnation of Acacius, who was responsible for the Henotikon,
and was the real cause of the severance between the
churches. The steps towards reunion may
be traced in the correspondence between
Hormisdas and Justinian. It was finally
achieved on the 27th of March, 519. The patriarch of
Constantinople declared that he held the Churches of
the old and the new Rome to be one; and with that
regard he accepted the four Councils and condemned
the heretics, including Acacius.

Reunion, 519.

The Church of Alexandria did not accept the reunion;
and Severus, patriarch of Antioch, was deposed for his
heresy. There was indeed a considerable party all over
the East which remained Monophysite; and this party
it was the first aim of Justinian (527–65), when he became emperor, to convince or to subdue. He was the

nephew of Justin, and he was already trained in the
work of government; but he seemed to be even more
zealous as a theologian than as a lawyer or administrator. The problem of Monophysitism fascinated him.
From the first, he applied himself seriously   The
to the study of the question in all its bear-   Emperor
ings. Night after night, says Procopius,   Justinian.
he would study in his library the writings of the
Fathers and the Holy Scriptures themselves, with some
learned monks or prelates with whom he might discuss
the problems which arose from their perusal. He had
all a lawyer's passion for definition, and all a theologian's delight in truth. And as year by year he
mastered the intricate arguments which had surged
round the decisions of the Councils, he came to consider
that a *rapprochement* was not impossible between the
Orthodox Church and those many Eastern monks and
prelates who still hesitated over a repudiation which
might mean heresy or schism. And from the first it
was his aim to unite not by arms but by arguments.
The incessant and wearisome theological discussions
which are among the most prominent features of his
reign, are a clearly intended part of a policy which was
to reunite Christendom and consolidate the definition
of the Faith by a thorough investigation of contro-
verted matters. Justinian first thought out vexed
questions for himself, and then endeavoured to make
others think them out.

From 527, in the East, Church history may be said to
start on new lines. The Catholic definition was completed and the imperial power was definitely committed
to it. We may now look at the Orthodox Church as
one, united against outside error.

A period of critical interest in the history of Europe is that to which belongs the difficult and complicated Church history of the East from the accession of the Emperor Justinian to the death of S. Methodius.

The period naturally divides itself into three parts —the first, from 527 to 628, dealing with the Church at the height of its authority, up to the overthrow of the Persian power; the second to 725, the period up to the beginning of the iconoclastic controversy; and the third up to its close and the death of S. Methodius in 847. With the first we will deal in the present chapter.

But throughout the whole three centuries, from 527 to 847, the essential character of the Church's **Church** life in the East is the same. In the East **and State** the Church was regarded more decisively **in the** than in the West as the complement of **East.** the State. Constantine had taught men to look for the officials of the Church side by side with those of the civil power. At Constantinople was the centre of an official Christianity, which recognised the powers that be as ordained of God in a way which was never found at Rome. At Rome the bishops came to be political leaders, to plot against governments, to found a political power of their own. At Constantinople the patriarchs, recognised as such by the Emperor and Senate of the New Rome, sought not to intrude themselves into a sphere outside their religious calling, but developed their claims, in their own sphere, side by side with those of the State; and their example was followed in the Churches which began to look to Constantinople for guidance. There was a necessary consequence of this.

It was that when the nationalities of the East,—in Egypt, Syria, Armenia, or even in Meso- **National-** potamia—began to resent the rule of the **ism of the** Empire, and struggled to express a patriot- **Churches.** ism of their own, they sought to express it also on the ecclesiastical side, in revolt from the Church which ruled as a complement to the civil power. Heresy came to be a sort of patriotism in religion. And while there was this of evil, it was not evil that each new barbarian nation, as it accepted the faith, sought to set up beside its own sovereign its patriarch also. "Imperium," they said, "sine patriarcha non staret," an adage which James I. of England inverted when he said, "No bishop, no king." Though the Bulgarians agreed with the Church of Constantinople in dogmas, they would not submit to its jurisdiction. The principle of national Churches, independent of any earthly supreme head, but united in the same faith and baptism, was established by the history of the East. Gradually the Church of Constantinople, by the growth of new Christian states, and by the defections of nations that had become heretical, became practically isolated, long before the infidels hedged in the boundaries of the Empire and hounded the imperial power to its death. Within the boundaries the Church continued to walk hand-in-hand with the State. Together they acted within and without. Within, they upheld the Orthodox Faith; without, they gave Cyprus its religious independence, Illyricum a new ecclesiastical organisation, the Sinaitic peninsula an autonomous hierarchy. More and more the history of these centuries shows us the Greek Church as the Eastern Empire in its religious aspect. And it shows that the division between East

and West, beginning in politics, was bound to spread
to religion. As Rome had won her ecclesiastical
primacy through her political position, so with Constantinople; and when the politics became divergent so
did the definition of faith. Rome, as a church, clung
to the obsolete claims which the State could no longer
enforce: Constantinople witnessed to the independence
which was the heritage of liberty given by the endow-
ment of Jesus Christ.

Such are the general lines upon which Eastern
Church history proceeds. We must now speak in more
detail, though briefly, of the theological history of the
years when Justinian was emperor.

Justinian was a trained theologian, but he was also a
trained lawyer; and the combination generally pro-
duces a vigorous controversialist. It was in controversy
that his reign was passed. The first controversy,
which began before he was emperor, was that, revived
Early con- from the end of the fifth century, which
troversy in dealt with the question of the addition to
Justinian's the Trisagion of the words, "Who was
reign. crucified for us," and involved the assertion
that One of the Trinity died upon the cross. In 519
there came from Tomi to Constantinople monks who
fancied that they could reconcile Christendom by adding to the Creed, a delusion as futile as that of those
who think they can advance towards the same end by
subtracting from it. After a debate on the matter in
Constantinople, Justinian consulted the pope. Letters
passed with no result. In 533, when the matter was
revived by the Akoimetai, Justinian published an edict
and wrote letters to pope and patriarch to bring the
matter to a final decision. "If One of the Trinity did

not suffer in the flesh, neither was He born in the flesh, nor can Mary be said, verily and truly, to be His Mother." The emperor himself was accused of heresy by the Vigilists; and at last Pope John II. declared the phrase, "One Person of the Trinity was crucified," to be orthodox. His judgment was confirmed by the Fifth General Council.[1]

The position which the emperor thus assumed was not one which the East alone welcomed. Rome, too, recognised that the East had power to make decrees, so long as they were consonant with apostolic doctrine.

The Monophysites.

Justinian now gave himself eagerly to the reconciliation of the Monophysites. In 535 Anthimus, bishop of Trebizond, a friend of the deposed patriarch of Antioch, Severus, who was at least semi-Monophysite, was elected to the patriarchal throne of New Rome. In the same year Pope Agapetus (534–6) came to Constantinople as an envoy of a Gothic king, and he demanded that Anthimus should make formal profession of orthodoxy. The result was not satisfactory: the new patriarch was condemned by the emperor with the sanction of the pope and the approval of a synod. Justinian then issued a decree condemning Monophysitism, which he ordered the new patriarch to send to the Eastern Churches. Mennas, the successor of Anthimus, in his local synod, had condemned and deposed the Monophysite bishops. The controversy was at an end.

More important in its results was the dispute with the so-called Origenists. S. Sabas came from Pales-

[1] Mansi, *Concilia*, ix. 384. The phrase was preserved in the Hymn Ὁ μονογενής, which was inserted in the Mass, and the composition of which is ascribed to Justinian himself.

tine in 531 to lay before the emperor the sad tale of the
spread of their evil doctrines, but he died in
The Origenists. the next year, and the Holy Land remained
the scene of strife between the two famous
monasteries of the Old and the New Laura. In 541
or 542 a synod at Antioch condemned the doctrines
of Origen, but the only result was that Jerusalem refused communion with the other Eastern patriarchate.
Justinian himself,—at a time when there was at Constantinople an envoy from Rome, Pelagius,—issued a
long declaration condemning Origen. A synod was
summoned, which formally condemned Origen in person—a precedent for the later anathemas of the Fifth
General Council—and fifteen propositions from his
writings, ten of them being those which Justinian's
edict had denounced. The decisions were sent for sub-
scription to the patriarchs of Alexandria, Antioch, and
Jerusalem, as well as to Rome. This sanction gave
something of an universal condemnation of Origenism;
but, since no general council confirmed it, it cannot be
asserted that Origen lies under anathema as a heretic.
The opinion of the legalists of the age was utterly out
of sympathy with one who was rather the cause of
heresy in others than himself heretical.

But the most important controversy of the reign was
that which was concerned with the "Three Chapters."
The "Three Chapters." Justinian, who had himself written against
the Monophysites, was led aside by an
ingenious monk into an attack upon the
writings of Theodore of Mopsuestia, Theodoret of
Cyrrhus, and Ibas of Edessa. The Emperor issued an
edict (544) in which "Three Chapters" asserted the
heresy of the incriminated writings. Within a short

time the phrase " The Three Chapters " was applied to
the subjects of the condemnation; and the Fifth
General Council, followed by later usage, describes
as the " Three Chapters" the " impious Theodore of
Mopsuestia with his wicked writings, and those things
which Theodoret impiously wrote, and the impious
letter which is said to be by Ibas."[1]

Justinian's edict was not favourably received: even
the patriarch Mennas hesitated, and the papal envoy.
and some African bishops broke off communion. The
Latin bishops rejected it; but the patriarchs of Alexandria, Antioch, and Jerusalem gave their adhesion.
Justinian summoned Pope Vigilius ; and a pitiable example of irresolution he presented when he came. He
accepted, rejected, censured, was complacent and hostile
in turns. At last he agreed to the summoning of a
General Council, and Justinian ordered it to meet in
May, 553. Vigilius, almost at the last moment, would
have nothing to do with it. The patriarch of Constantinople presided, and the patriarchs of Antioch and
Alexandria appeared in person, the patriarch of Jerusalem by three bishops. The acts of the Council were
signed by 164 prelates. The Council, like its predecessors, was predominantly Eastern; but its decisions
were afterwards accepted by the West. The precedents
of the earlier Councils were strictly followed   **The Fifth**
in regard to Rome: no supremacy was allow-   **General**
ed, though the honourable primacy was not   **Council,**
contested.[2] Justinian's letter, sketching   **553.**
the history of the controversy of the Three Chapters,

[1] Mansi, ix. 181.

[2] Cf. Nicaea, Canon vi. ; Constantinople, Canons ii. and iii. ;
Ephesus, Canon viii. ; Chalcedon, Canons ix. and xvii.

C

was read, but he did not interfere with the delibera-
tions.   It was summoned to deal with matters concerning the faith, and these were always left to the
decision of the Episcopate.   The discussion was long;
and after an exhaustive examination of the writings of
Theodore, the Council proceeded to endorse the first
"chapter," by the condemnation of the Mopsuestian
and his writings.   The case of Theodoret was less
clear: indeed, a very eminent authority has regarded
the action of the Council in his case as "not quite
equitable." [1]   But the grounds of the condemnation
were such statements of his as that " God the Word is
not incarnate," " we do not acknowledge an hypostatic
union," and his description of S. Cyril as *impius, im-
pugnator Christi, novus haereticus*, with a denial of the
communicatio idiomatum, which left little if any doubt
as to his own position.[2]   When the letter of Ibas came
to be considered, it was plainly shown that its statements were directly contrary to the affirmations of
Chalcedon.   It denied the Incarnation of the Word,
refused the title of Theotokos to the Blessed Virgin,
and condemned the doctrines of Cyril.   The Council
had no hesitation in saying anathema.

Here its work was ended.   It had safeguarded the
faith by definitely exposing the logical consequences of
statements which indirectly impugned the Divine and
Human Natures of the Incarnate Son.

The need for its decisions.   So long as human progress is based upon
intellectual principles as well as on material
growth, a teaching body which professes to
guard and interpret a Divine Revelation must speak

[1] Dr. W. Bright, *Waymarks in Church History*, p. 238.
[2] See Hefele, *History of the Councils* (Eng. trans.), iv. 311.

without hesitation when its "deposit" is attacked. The Church has clung, with an inspired sagacity, to the reality of the Incarnation : and thus it has preserved to humanity a real Saviour and a real Exemplar. The subtle brains which during these centuries searched for one joint in the Catholic armour wherein to insert a deadly dart, were foiled by a subtlety as acute, and by deductions and definitions that were logical, rational, and necessary. If the Councils had not defined the faith which had been once for all delivered to the saints, it would have been dissolved little by little by sentimental concessions and shallow inconsistencies of interpretation. It was the work of the Councils to develope and apply the principles furnished by the sacred Scriptures. New questions arose, and it was necessary to meet them : it was clear, then, that there was a real division between those who accepted Christianity in the full logical meaning of the Scriptures, in the full confidence of the Church, and those who doubted, hesitated, denied; and it is clear now that the whole future of Christendom depended upon the acceptance by the Christian nations of a single rational and logically tenable Creed. This involved the rejection of the Three Chapters, as it involved equally the condemnation of Monophysitism and Monothelitism. From the point of view of theology or philosophy the value of the work of the Church in this age is equally great. The heresies which were condemned in the sixth century (as in the seventh) were such as would have utterly destroyed the logical and rational conception of the Person of the Incarnate Son, as the Church had received it by divine inspiration. Some Christian historians may seem for a moment to yield a half assent to the shallow opinions of those who would refuse to go beyond what is sometimes strangely called the "primitive simplicity of the Gospel." But it is impossible in this obscurantist fashion to check the free inquiry of the human intellect. The truths of the Gospel must be studied and pondered over, and set in their proper relation to each other. There must be logical inferences from them, and reasonable conclusions. It is this which explains that struggle for the Catholic Faith of which historians are sometimes impatient, and justifies a high estimate of the services which the Church of Constantinople rendered to the Church Universal.

It is in this light that the work of the Fifth General Council, to be truly estimated, must be regarded. It will be convenient here to summarise the steps by which the Fifth General Council won recognition in the Church.

In the first place, the emperor, according to custom, confirmed what the Council had decreed; and throughout the greater part of the East the decision of Church and State alike was accepted. In 553 there was a formal confirmation by a synod of bishops at Jerusalem; but for the most part there was no need of such pronouncement. African bishops and Syrian monks here and there refused obedience; but the Church as a whole was agreed.

Pope Vigilius, it would seem, was in exile for six months on an island in the Sea of Marmora. On December 8, 553, he formally anathematised the Three Chapters. On February 23, 554, in a *Constitution*, he announced to the Western bishops his adhesion to the decisions

Pope Vigilius.

of the General Council. Before the end of 557 he was succeeded, on his death, by Pelagius, well known in Constantinople. He, like Vigilius, had once refused but now accepted the Council.

When Rome and Constantinople were agreed, the adhesion of the rest of the Catholic world was only a question of time. But the time was long. In North Italy there was for long a practical schism, which was not healed till Justin II. issued an explanatory edict,[1] and the genius, spiritual and diplomatic, of Gregory the Great was devoted to the task of conciliation. Still it was not till the very beginning of the eighth century [2] that the last schismatics returned to union with the Church : thus a division in the see of Aquileia, by which for a time there were two rival patriarchates, was closed. Already the rest of Europe had come to peace.

The last years of Justinian were disturbed by a new heresy, that of those who taught that the Body of the Lord was incorruptible, and it was asserted that the emperor himself fell into this error. The evidence is slight and contradictory, and the matter is of no importance in the general history of the Church.[3] But it is worth remembering that little more than a century after his death his name was singled out by the Sixth General Council for special honour as of " holy memory." His work, indeed, had been great, as theologian and as Christian emperor ; there was no more important or more accurate writer

The
Aphtharto-
docetes.

[1] Given in Evagrius, v. 4.
[2] A.D. 700, Mansi, Concilia, xii. 115.
[3] See Gibbon, ed. J. B. Bury, vol. v. pp. 139, 140, 522, 523 ; and W. H. Hutton, The Church of the Sixth Century, pp. 204–240, 303–309.

on theology in the East during the sixth century; and he must ever be remembered side by side with the Fifth General Council which he summoned. There were many defects in the Eastern theory of the relations between Church and State; but undoubtedly under such an emperor it had its best chances of success.

Justinian has been declared to have forced upon the Empire which he had reunited the orthodoxy of **The** S. Cyril and the Council of Chalcedon, and **work of** the attempt has been made to prove that **Justinian,** Cyril himself was a Monophysite.[1] The best refutation of this view is the perfect harmony of the decisions of the Fifth General Council with those of the previous Œcumenical assemblies, and the fact that no novelty could be discovered to have been added to "the Faith" when the "Three Chapters" were condemned.

With the close of the Council the definition of Christian doctrine passes into the background till the rise of the Monothelite controversy. When its decisions were accepted, the labours of Justinian had given peace to the churches.

From 565, when Justinian died, to 628, when Heraclius freed the Empire from the danger of Persian conquest, were years of comparative rest in **and his** the Church. It was a period of missionary **successors.** extension, of quiet assertion of spiritual authority, in the midst of political trouble and disaster. Gibbon, who asserts that Justinian died a heretic, adds, "The reigns of his four successors, Justin, Tiberius, Maurice, and Phocas, are distinguished by a rare, though fortunate, vacancy in the ecclesiastical history

[1] Cf. Harnack, *Dogmengeschichte*, ii. pp. 395, 396, 399, etc.

of the East"; and the sarcasm, though not wholly accurate, may serve to express the gradual progress of unity which marked the years up to the accession of Heraclius. The history of religion is concerned rather with those outside than those within the Church. That history we need not follow, and we may pass over this period with only a brief allusion to the development of independence outside the immediate range of the ecclesiastical power of New Rome. Heresies grew as an expression of national independence. The Chaldæan Church, which stretched to Persia and India, was Nestorian. The Monophysites won the Coptic Church of Egypt, the Abyssinian Church, the Jacobites in Syria, the Armenians in the heart of Asia Minor. In the mountains of Lebanon the Monothelites—of whom we have to speak shortly —organised the Maronite Church ; and in Georgia the Church was aided by geographical conditions as well as historical development to ignore the overlordship of the Church of Antioch. So in Europe grew up with the new States, the Bulgarian, the Serbian, and the Wallachian Churches.

Rise of separated bodies.

It was thus that, alike as statesmen and Christians, the emperors were devoted advocates of missions. Their wars of conquest often—as notably with the great Emperor Heraclius—assumed and the character of holy wars. Where the barbarians of the East made havoc there too often the Church fell without leaving a trace of its work. Without priest and sacrament, the people came to retain only among their superstitions, as sometimes in North Africa to-day, usages which showed that once their ancestors belonged to the kingdom of Christ. Much

Missions and failures.

of the missionary work of the period was done by
Monophysites; the record of John of Ephesus preserves what he himself did to spread Christianity in
Asia. And it would seem that even the most orthodox
of emperors was willing to aid in the work of those
who did not accept the Council of Chalcedon so long
as they earnestly endeavoured to teach the heathen
the rudiments of the faith and to love the Lord in
incorruptness.

The Church of the period was divided into five
patriarchates, the Church of Cyprus being understood
Organisa- to stand apart and autocephalous. Rome,
tion of the Constantinople, Alexandria, Antioch still
Church. retained their old power, while Jerusalem
was regarded as somewhat inferior. The patriarchates were divided into provinces, the capital of
each province having its metropolitan bishop. Under
him were other bishops, and gradually the title of
archbishop was being understood,—as by Justinian
in the decree (Novel. xi.) in which he created his
birthplace a metropolitan see,—to imply jurisdiction
over a number of suffragan sees. Besides this there
were still sees autocephalous in the sense that they
owned no superior or metropolitan bishop. It would
seem from the *Synekdemos* of Hierocles (*c.* 535)
that in the sixth century the patriarch of Constantinople had under him about thirty metropolitans and
some 450 bishops. But the authority which the
patriarch exercised was by no means used to minimise
that of the bishops. If the influence of the Imperial
Court on the patriarchate was always considerable
and sometimes overwhelming, Justinian was careful
to preserve the independence of the Episcopate and

to order that the first steps in the election of bishops should be by the clergy and the chief citizens in each diocese. And, as a letter of S. Gregory shows, the bishops were elected for life; neither infirmity nor old age was regarded as a cause for deposition, and translation from see to see was condemned by many a Council. All the clergy under the rank of bishop might marry, but only before ordination to the higher orders. In the East it would seem that the number of persons connected in some way with ecclesiastical office was very large. Even excluding the monks,— a numerous and continually increasing body — the hermits, the Stylites (who remained for years on a pillar, where they even received Communion, in a special vessel made for the purpose), the different orders of celibate women—there was still a very considerable number of persons attached to all the important churches, in different positions of ministry. The famous poem of Paul the Silentiary on S. Sophia revels in a recital of the number of persons employed as well as in the beauty of the magnificent building itself.

In architecture, indeed, the Byzantine Church of the sixth century was supreme. No more glorious edifice has ever been consecrated to the service of Christ than the Church of the Divine Wisdom at Constantinople; and the arts which enriched it in mosaic, marble, metals, were brought to a perfection which excited the wonder of succeeding centuries. Before we end this sketch of the history of a great age in the life of the Eastern Church, a word must be said about its most splendid and enduring memorial. Among the most striking passages in the

chronicles of the age are the famous descriptions by
S. Sophia Procopius and by Paul the Silentiary of
at Constan- the splendours of the great church of Con-
tinople. stantinople in the sixth century after
Christ. In the wonderful art of mosaic, as it
may be seen to-day in some of the churches of the
New Rome, in S. Sophia—though much there is still
covered—and in the Church of the Chora, the West,
with all the beauty that we may still see in Ravenna,
was never able to equal the East. In solemn grandeur
of architecture fitted for open, public, common worship,
expressive of the profoundest verities of Christ's
Church, it would be difficult to surpass the work of
the great age of Byzantine art. Of this S. Sophia,
the Church of the Divine Wisdom, at Constantinople,
built by the architects of the Emperor Justinian in the
sixth century, is the most magnificent example. There
the eye travels upward, when the great nave is entered
from the narthex, from the arches supporting the
gallery to those of the gallery itself, from semi-domes
larger and larger, up to the great dome itself, an
intricate scheme merging in a central unity. "The
length and the breadth and the height of it are
equal" is the exclamation which seems forced from
the beholder : never was there a church so vast yet so
symmetrical, so admirably designed for the participa-
tion of all worshippers in the great act of worship. And
the splendid pillars, brought from Baalbek of the old
heathen days, wrought on the capitals with intricate
carvings, with emblems and devices and monograms,
the finely decorated doors, and the gigantic mosaic
seraphim on the walls, still in the twentieth century
dimly image something of the glowing worship of the

sixth. Then the "splendour of the lighted space," glittering with thousands of lights, gave "shine unto the world," and guided the seafarers as they went forth " by the divine light of the Church itself." Traveller after traveller, chronicler after chronicler, records impressions of the glory and beauty that belonged to the great Mother Church of the Byzantine rite. Historically, perhaps no church in the world has seen, at least in the Middle Ages, so many scenes that belonged to the deepest crises of national life. From the day when the great emperor who built it prostrated himself before God as unworthy to make the offering of so much beauty, to the day when Muhammad the conqueror (says the legend) rode in over the heaps of Christian dead, it was the centre, and the mirror, of the Church's life in the capital of the Empire. And that is what the worship of the East has always striven to express. It is immemorial, conservative beyond anything that the West can tolerate or conceive; but it belongs, in the present as in the past, to the closest thoughts, the most intimate experiences, of men to whom religion is indeed the guide of life. The Church of S. Sophia, the worship of the East, are the living memorials of the great age of the great Christian emperor and theologian of the sixth century.

And the fact that this building was due to the genius and power not of the Church, but of Justinian, leads us back to the significance of the State authority in the ecclesiastical history of the East.

As it was said in England that kings were the Church's nursing fathers, so in the Eastern Empire might the same text be used in rather a different sense. The Church was in power before the Empire was Christian; but the Christian Empire was ever urgent to proclaim its attachment to the Church and to guarantee its protection. The imperial legislation of the great lawgiver began always in the name of the Lord, and the code emphasised as the foundation of society and civil law the orthodox doctrines of the Trinity and of Christ. And step by step the great emperor endeavoured, in matters of morality and of gambling, to enforce the moral laws of the Church. Works of charity and mercy were undertaken by Church and State, hand in hand, and the noble buildings which marked the magnificent period of Byzantine architecture were the works of a society which, from the highest to the lowest member, was penetrated by Christian ideals. Thus, very briefly, we may epitomise the work of the first period we have mentioned. A word must be said later of later times.

CHAPTER III

THE CHURCH IN ITALY, 461–590

THE death of S. Leo took place but a few years before the Roman Empire in the West became extinguished, and political interests entirely submerged those of religion in the years that followed it. Dimly, beneath the noise of the barbarian triumph, we discern the survival in Rome of the Church's powers and claims; but it is not till the rise of another pope of mighty genius that they claim any consideration as important. In 461 died S. Leo; in 476 Romulus Augustulus, the last of the continuous line of Western Caesars, surrendered his sceptre to the Herul Odowakar. The barbarian governed with the aid of Roman statesmen: he fixed his seat of rule at Ravenna rather than at Rome: he showed consideration to the saintly Epiphanius, Bishop of Pavia: heretic though he was, he desired to keep well with the Catholic bishops of Rome. After him came a greater man, Theodoric the Goth, whose capture of Ravenna, March 5th, 493, was followed by the assassination of Odowakar. Theodoric, also an Arian, became sole ruler of Italy. He too was served by Roman officials, and his administration was modelled on that of the Caesars. A special interest attaches to his

The end of the Empire in the West, 476.

Theodoric the Goth, 493.

29

dealings with the Church. The king, indeed, Arian though he was, looked on the Catholic Church with no unfriendly eye. His great minister, Cassiodorus, was orthodox : and it is in his writings, which enshrine the policy of his master, that we must search for the relations between Church and State in the days before Belisarius had won back Ravenna and Italy to the allegiance of the Roman Cæsar.

The letters of Cassiodorus supply, if not a complete account, at least very valuable illustrations, of the position assumed by the East Gothic power under Theodoric and his successors in regard to the Church. The favour shown by the Ostrogoth sovereign to Cassiodorus, a staunch Catholic, yet senator, consul, patrician, quæstor, and prætorian præfect, is in itself an illustration of the absence of bitter Arian feeling. This impression is deepened by a perusal of the letters which Cassiodorus wrote in the name of his sovereign. The subjects in which the Church is most frequently related to the State are jurisdiction and property. In the latter there seems a clear desire on the part of the kings to give security and to act even with generosity to all religious bodies, Catholic as well as Arian. Church property was frequently, if not always, freed from taxation.[1] The principle which dictated the whole policy of Theodoric is to be seen in a letter to Adila, senator and comes.[2] "Although we will not that any should suffer any wrong whom it belongs to our religious obligation to protect, since the free tranquillity of the subjects is the glory of the ruler; yet especially do we desire that all churches

His relation with the Catholic Church.

. [1] So *Var.*, i. 26, ed. Mommsen, p. 28.   [2] ii. 29, p. 63.

should be free from any injury, since while they are in peace the mercy of.God is bestowed on us." There- fore he orders all protection to be given to the churches: yet answer is to be made in the law courts to any suit against them. For, as he says in another letter, "if false claims may not be tolerated against men, how much less against God." Again, "If we are willing to enrich the Church by our own liberality, *a fortiori* will we not allow it to be despoiled of the gifts received from pious princes in the past."

It was on such liberality that the material power of the Church was slowly strengthening itself. Simi- larly, as in the East, clerical privilege was beginning to be allowed in the law courts : the Church was acquiring the right to judge all cases in which her officers were concerned. Theodoric's successors bettered his instructions. Athalaric allowed to the Roman pope the jurisdiction over all suits affecting the Roman clergy.

But this picture of toleration and privilege which we obtain from the official letters of Cassiodorus, cannot be regarded as a complete description of the Weakness attitude of the East Gothic rule towards of the the Catholic Church. Pope after pope was Church. the humble slave of the Gothic ruler. They were sent to Constantinople as his envoys, and though they stood firm for the Catholic faith and in rejection of all com- promise with regard to the doctrine of Chalcedon, they were entirely impotent in Italy itself. Catholic Italy was at the feet of the Arian Goth. The cruel im- prisonment of Pope John, used as a political tool in 525 and flung away when he proved ineffective, gave a new martyr to the Roman calendar ; and, in spite of the absence of direct evidence, it is difficult to regard the executions of Symmachus and of Boethius as entirely unconnected with religious questions. Both were Catholics; both, to use Mr. Hodgkin's words,[1] "have been surrounded by a halo of fictitious sanctity as martyrs to the cause of Christian orthodoxy." The father-in-law, "lest, through grief for the loss of his son-in-law, he should attempt anything against his kingdom," Theodoric "caused to be accused and ordered him to be slain."[2] Boethius, who wrote the most famous work of the Early Middle Age, *The Consolation of Philosophy*, a book which became the delight of Christian scholars, of monks and kings, was translated by Alfred the West Saxon, and formed the foundation of very much of the Christian thought of many succeeding generations, met a horrible death in 526 on a charge of corresponding with the orthodox Emperor Justin. No doubt the main reason for the butchery was political; but it is impossible in this age wholly to separate religion from politics; especially when we read, in almost immediate conjunction with the story of the murder of these men, that Theodoric ordered that on a certain day the Arians should take possession of all the Catholic basilicas. It was not until the Gothic power had finally fallen, and Narses had re-established the imperial power, that the life and property of Catholics were absolutely safe.

The death of Theodoric (August 30, 526) was followed by the downfall of his power. Within ten years all Italy was won back to the Roman and Catholic Empire ruling from the East.

[1] *Italy and her Invaders*, vol. iii. p. 516.
Anonymus Valesii.

With the restoration of the imperial power the Church came to the front more prominently. So long as Justinian reigned the popes were kept in subjection; but ecclesiastics generally were admitted to a large share in judicial and political power. The emperors looked for their strongest political support in the Catholic party. Suppression of Arianism became a political necessity at Ravenna. Justinian gave to Agnellus the churches of the Arians. In 554 the emperor issued his solemn Pragmatic Sanction for the government of Italy. Of this, Section XII. gives a power to the bishops which shows the intimate connection between State and Church. "Moreover we order that fit and proper persons, able to administer the local government, be chosen as *iudices* of the provinces by the bishops and chief persons of each province from the inhabitants of the province itself." This is important, of course, as allowing popular elections, but far more important in its recognition of the position of the clerical estate. Justinian's new administration of Italy was to be military; but hardly less was it to be ecclesiastical. Here we have, says Mr. Hodgkin,[1]—whose words I quote because I can find none better to express what seems to me to be the significance of this act—"a pathetic confession of the emperor's own inability to cope with the corruption and servility of his civil servants. He seems to have perceived that in the great quaking bog of servility and dishonesty by which he felt himself to be surrounded, his only sure standing-ground was to be found in the spiritual estate, the order of men who wielded a power

The imperial restoration, 554.

The Pragmatic Sanction.

---

[1] *Italy and her Invaders*, vol. vi. p. 523.

D

not of this world, and who, if true to their sacred mission, had nothing to fear and little to hope from the corrupt minions of the court." This is significant in regard to the rise of the power of the popes in the Western capital of the Empire and in the whole of Italy. It was by the good deeds of the clergy, and by the need of them, that they came forward before long as the masters of the country.

This rule of the Pragmatic Sanction was not an isolated instance ; at every point the bishop was placed *en rapport* with the State, with the provincials, and with the exarch himself.[1] In jurisdiction, in advice, from the moment when he assisted at a new governor's installation, the bishop was at the side of the lay officer, to complain and even, if need be, to control.

One power still remained to the emperor himself (in the seventh century it was transferred to the exarch) —that of confirming the election of the pope. Narses seated Pelagius on the papal throne ; but when one as mighty as the "eunuch general" arose in Gregory the Great, the power of the exarchate passed, slowly but surely, into the hands of the papacy. The changes of rulers in Italy, the policies of the falling Goths and of the rising Roman Empire, found their completion in the effects of the Lombard invasion. But before this there were thirty years of growth for the Church, and the growth was due very largely to a new force, though for a while it remained below the surface. It was the power of the monastic life, realised anew by the genius and holiness of S. Benedict of Nursia.

---

[1] Instances are collected by M. Diehl, *Études sur l'administration byzantine dans l'exarchat de Ravenne*, p. 320.

Born about 480, of noble parentage, he gave himself
from early years to serve God "in the
desert." At about the age of fifteen he is
spoken of by his biographer, the great
S. Gregory, in words which might form the motto
of his life, as "sapienter indoctus." First, a solitary
at Subiaco; then the unwilling abbat of a neighbouring
monastery, whose monks endeavoured to kill him;
then again living "by himself in the sight of Him
who seeth all things"; at last, in 529, he founded
in Campania the monastery of Monte Cassino, the
mother of all the revived monasticism of the Middle
Age.

The work of S. Benedict.

The monastery of Monte Cassino became a pattern
of the religious life. S. Benedict was a wise and
statesmanlike ruler, to whom men came with
confidence from every rank and every race,
to be his disciples, or to place their boys under him
for instruction. The rule which he drew up was
as potent in the ecclesiastical world as was the code
of Justinian in the civil. It had its bases in the root
ideas of obedience, simplicity, and labour. "Never to
depart from the governance of God" was his primary
maxim to his monks; and a monastery was to be a
"school of the Lord's service" and a "workshop of the
spiritual art." The beginning of all was to be prayer.
"Inprimis ut quidquid agendum inchoas bonum, a
Deo perfici instantissima oratione deposcas." And
though absolute power was left, without appeal, in the
hands of the abbat, and the rule of the whole house
was to be "nullus in monasterio proprii sequatur
cordis voluntatem," yet great individual liberty was
left to each monk in the direction of his own religious

His rule.

life.   Everyone, he knew, had "his own gift of God"—
some could fast more than others; some could spend
more time in silent prayer and meditation; and none
could do any good, he knew, however strict their outer
rule, without daily enlightenment from God.   There
was place in his scheme for those whose work was
chiefly manual, those who reclaimed uncultivated lands
and turned the wilderness into a garden of the Lord,
and for those who spent long hours in contemplation
and prayer.   The public solemn singing of offices was
no more characteristic of his rule than was the following of the hermits in pure prayer.

One who would be admitted to the monastery must
take oath before the whole community that he intended constantly to remain firm in his profession, to
live a life of conversion to God, and to obey those set
over him, but the last only "according to the rule."
True monks were his followers to count themselves
only if they lived by the labours of their hands.
Idleness, said Benedict, is the enemy of the soul.   The
life of the monks was ascetic, but without the extreme
rigour of the earlier "religious"—hermits and cœno-
bites.   The rule required austerities, and gave strict
injunction as to food at all times, and especially in
Lent; but it did not encourage voluntary austerities
beyond the rule, and it admitted many relaxations
for the old, the infirm, or those whose labours were
especially hard.

Where all depended so much on a superior it was
of especial importance that he should be wisely chosen
and should rule wisely.   In three things he was to be
pre-eminent—exhortation, example, and prayer; and
prayer, says the saint, is the greatest of these; for

although there be much virtue in exhortation and
example, yet prayer is that which promotes grace
and efficacy alike in deed and word. He was to
recognise no difference of social rank. Good deeds
and obedience were to be the only ways to his favour.
Only if exceptional merit required promotion was
there to be any breach of the proper order in which
each should hold his place, "since, whether slaves
or free, we are all one in Christ, and, under the same
Lord, wear all of us the same badge of service."

In a cell hard by the monastery dwelt Benedict's
sister, S. Scholastica, whose religious life he directed, but
whom he rarely saw, and who became a pattern to
nuns as he to monks.

The influence of Benedict was, even in his own life-
time, extraordinary. There were times when it might
almost be said that all Italy looked to him
for guidance; and there is no more striking   **Its wide
influence.**
scene in the history of the decaying Gothic
power than when the cruel Totila, whose end he
foresaw, and the secrets of whose heart lay open to
his gaze, visited him in his monastery and heard the
words of truth from his lips. When, fortified by the
Body and Blood of the Lord, he passed away with
hands still uplifted in prayer, he had created a power
which did more than any other to make the Church
predominant in Italy. The rule, the definite organisations, of monasticism came to the world from Italy
and from Benedict. Though the Benedictines were
never actively papal agents, yet indirectly, by their
training and by their influence on the whole nature
of medieval religion, they formed a strong support
for the growing power of the Roman see.

But Benedict was not the only leader, though he was the greatest, in the monastic revival of the sixth century. With another great name his work may be placed to some extent in contrast.

S. Benedict was no advocate of exclusively ecclesiastical study. He adapted the ancient literatures to the Scholarship and learning. purposes of Christian education. It is true that the main subjects of study for his monks were the Holy Scriptures, and the chief object the edification of the individual by meditation and of the people by preaching; but the monks learnt to write verse correctly and prose in what had claims to be considered a style. Yet what he himself did in that direction was little indeed. Perhaps the most that can be said is that he left the way open to his successors. And of these the greatest was Cassiodorus.

Cassiodorus, the statesman, the orthodox adviser and friend of the Arian Theodoric, lived to become a Christian teacher and a monk. The friend Cassiodorus. of Pope Agapetus, he endeavoured with his sanction in 535 to set up a school in Rome which should give to Christians "a liberal education." The pope's death, a year later, prevented the scheme being carried out. But a few years later, in the monastery of Vivarium near Squillace, he set himself to found a religious house which should preserve the ancient culture. Based on a sound knowledge of grammar, on a collation and correction of texts, on a study of ancient models in prose and verse, he would raise an education through "the arts and disciplines of liberal letters," for, he said, " by the study of secular literature our minds are trained to understand the Scriptures

themselves." That was the supreme end at Squillace,
as it was at Monte Cassino; and though Cassiodorus
looked at letters differently from Benedict, his work,
too, was important in founding a tradition for Italian
monasticism.

While monasticism was transforming Italy and
placing Catholicism on a firm basis in the Western
lands of the Empire, the power of the papal
see, when Rome was reconquered by the
imperial forces from Constantinople, seemed
to sink to the lowest depths. The papacy
under Vigilius (537-55) and Pelagius (555-
60) was the servant of the Byzantine Caesars. The
history of the controversies in which each pope was
engaged, the scandal of their elections, there is no need
to relate here. Suffice it to say that the decisions of
the Fifth General Council were in no way the work
of either, but were eventually accepted by both. The
self-contradictions of Vigilius are pitiable ; and the
acceptance of Pelagius by the Romans was only won by
his rejecting a formal statement of his predecessor.

Consecrated only by two bishops [1] on Easter Day,
556, he began a pontificate which was from the first
disputed and even despised. The Archbishop of Milan
and the patriarch of Aquileia would not communicate
with him. In Gaul he was received with suspicion, and
he was obliged to write to King Childebert, submitting
to him a profession of his faith.[2] It is clear that the
Gallican Church no more than the Lombard regarded

Weakness
of the
papacy
under
Pelagius,
555-60.

[1] Et dum non essent episcopi qui eum ordinarent, inventi sunt duo
episcopi, Johannes de Perusia et Bonus de Ferentino, et Andreas pres-
biter de Hostis, et ordinaverunt eum.—*Liber Pontificalis*, i. 303.
[2] Migne, *Patr. Lat.*, tom. lxix. p. 402.

the pope as *ipso facto* orthodox or the guardian of
orthodoxy. Even this letter of Pelagius was not regarded as satisfactory. It was long before the Churches
entered into communion with him ; and even to the
last, the northern sees of Italy refused. He ruled,
unquietly enough, for four years ; and died, leaving a
memory free at least from simony, and honoured as
a lover of the poor.

Under him, as under Vigilius, the papacy had been
compelled to submit to the judgment of the East.
"The Church of Rome," says Mgr. Duchesne, "was
humiliated." [1]

The lives of these two popes cover the most important period in the ecclesiastical history of the sixth
century. After the death of Pelagius I., and up to the
accession of Gregory the Great in 590, the interest of
Italian history is political rather than ecclesiastical.
The emperors tried to rule, through their exarchs at
Ravenna, from Constantinople. The papacy grew
quietly in power. Then came the Lombards and a new
era began.

[1] *Revue des Questions Historiques*, Oct. 1884, p. 439.

CHAPTER IV

CHRISTIANITY IN GAUL FROM THE SIXTH TO THE EIGHTH CENTURY

A VERY special interest belongs to the history of Christianity in Gaul. There is no more striking example of what the Church did to bridge over the gulf between the old culture and the barbarians.

Among early Christian martyrs few are more renowned than those who died in Southern Gaul. Paganism lived on, concealed, in many country districts, but the life and power and thought of the people became by the time of Constantine, by the fourth century, entirely Christian. As the state organised so did the Church. Gaul had seventeen provincial governments; it came to have seventeen archbishops, and under them bishops for each great city. On the Roman empire and the Christian Church the foundations were laid; and they were laid firm.

At the beginning of the fifth century a terrible storm swept over the land. It was the storm of Teutonic invasion. Vandals, Burgundians, Alans, Suevi poured over the land; the Huns followed them, only to be beaten back by a union of the other tribes. Then, after the Battle of Châlons (451), there gradually rose out

41

of the Teutonic conquerors the conquering power of one tribe, that of the Franks.

By the first ten years of the sixth century Gaul was united again, under the rule of Chlodowech **The** (Clovis), King of the Franks. Till well on **Church** in the Middle Ages it was that title which **in Gaul.** the rulers of Gaul always bore, " Rex Francorum," King of the Franks. France to-day still dates her existence as a nation from the baptism of Clovis. It was that, his admission into the Catholic Christianity of the Gauls over whom he ruled, which enlisted on the side of the Frankish power all the culture and civilisation which had never died out since the Roman days. Under the fostering care of the Church it had survived. Brotherhood, charity, compassion, unity, all the great ideas which the Church cherished, were to work in long ages the transformation of the Frankish kingship. And when Chlodowech became king under the blessing of the Church, which had survived all through these centuries since it was planted under the Romans, the fusion of races soon followed. The French nation as we now know it is not merely Celtic, or Gaulish, but Roman too, and lastly Frankish—that is, Teutonic.

The history of the baptism of Chlodowech is one of the most dramatic in the annals of the early Middle Age. **The** His wife, Chrotechild, was the niece of the **baptism of** Burgundian king, and she was a devout **Chlodo-** Catholic. Slowly she won her way to his **wech, 496.** heart. Never, said the chroniclers, did she cease to persuade him that he should serve the true God; and when in the crisis of a battle against the Alamanni he called her words to mind, he vowed to be baptised if Christ should give him the victory. The legend adorns the historic fact that Chlodowech was baptised by S. Remigius at Rheims, on Christmas Day, 496, and that some three thousand of his warriors were baptised with him. " Bow thy neck, O Sigambrian," said the prelate, " adore that which thou hast burned and burn that which thou hast adored." Within a generation all races of the Franks had followed the Frankish king.

The years that followed were full of growth. But for long the Christianity which was nominally triumphant was imperfect indeed. Chlodo- The dark wech died in 511; his race went on ruling, days of Catholic in name but very far from obedi- the Mer- ent to the Church's laws. The tale of wings. their successors, their wars and their crimes, is one which belongs to social or political history, not to the history of the Church. The Church's life was lived underground in the slow progress of Christian ideas. Chlothochar, sole ruler of the Franks, died in 561. How little had the half-century accomplished. Then came an age of division, murders, horrors, in which the names of great ladies stand out as at least the equals of their lords in crime. Fredegund, who became the wife of Chilperich of Neustria, and Bruni-childis, the wife first of Sigebert of Austrasia, and then of Merovech, Chilperich's son, were rivals in wickedness. The horrors of those days are recorded in the history of Gregory, who ruled over the see of Tours from 573 to 595. It was an age in which, while the rulers were Christian in name, and the land was mapped out into sees ruled by Christian bishops, and monasteries were springing up to teach the young and to set an example of religious life, the general atmosphere was almost avowedly pagan. Men said, tells Gregory, that "if a man has to pass between pagan altars and God's church there is no harm in his paying homage to both," and the lives of such men showed that it is impossible to serve God and Mammon.

Yet for a century and a half the Merwings, descendants of Chlodowech, had among them strong rulers, great conquerors, men of iron as well as men of blood. Early in the seventh century, from 628 to 638, there ruled in Gaul Dagobert, the greatest of the Merwing kings. His rule extended from the Pyrenees to the North Sea, from the ocean to the forests of Thuringia and Bohemia. He was "ruler of all Gaul and the greater part of Germany, very influential in the affairs of Spain, victorious over Slavs and Bulgarians, and at home a great king, encouraging commerce and putting into better shape the law codes of his subjects."

That was the culmination of the Merwing power. The seventh century saw its decay, and a new step **Break up** towards the medieval monarchy of the **of their** Franks. Two causes effected the fall of the **kingdom.** Merwings—their own vices and the growth of feudalism with the creation of great local lords. These threatened to break up the kingdom of Chlodowech into small states, to disintegrate and thus destroy the united nation of the Franks.

The first cause is one which it is difficult to exaggerate. We read in the pages of that great historian and great bishop, Gregory of Tours, the terrible tale of their crimes, their brutal luxury, their lust for blood, the

unbridled licence of their passions. That was the
record of the days of their decay. There was, however,
even at the best a great change from the times of
Roman rule. For civilisation, literary culture, law, we
find substituted in the pages of Gregory of Tours
savagery, scenes of brutality, drunkenness, robbery.
Law and civilisation seem to sleep. It was in this
state of the country, when every man's hand was
against his neighbour, when law was unheard amid the
strife, that feudalism arose, a natural development
of the desire for self-preservation, which led to associations to supply the mutual protection which there
was no strength behind the law to enforce. In all
these movements the Church had an active part. It
was her principles of association which taught men the
idea of unity, of bonds by which personal   The
security should be based on new guarantees   influence
amid the weakness of government and the   of the
neglect of law. The Church held the tradi-   Church.
tion of a civilisation the barbarians had never known,
and in her own moral teaching she set forth the
way to an ideal state which should combine all the
elements of strength. The growth of the Frankish
nation was guided almost entirely by the Church.

Feudalism, Roman administration and law, Christian
faith and discipline—these three factors were at work
throughout the Dark Ages from the fifth to the ninth
century: and they were all—the last two most
especially—under the direction of the Church. And
first and most obviously the monarchy of the Merwings
was a patent imitation of the Roman Empire. The
clergy had maintained the imperial tradition. It was
they who taught the sovereigns to replace the emperors

and to produce around them the illusion of a Roman rule. They employed officers with the same titles, centred their administration in their household, claimed and exercised unlimited power. No power above them did they recognise, save only, when they would listen to their teachers, the power of the love—more often the fear—of God. The barbarian invasions that had swept over the land had destroyed the local, as well as the central administration. At Arles survived the relics of the old Roman functionaries of the prefecture; but in the land of the Franks the whole system had to be reconstructed from the tradition of which the Church was the faithful guardian.

Thus the real aim of Chlodowech and his successors was not to conquer the Roman Empire, not to substitute a Teutonic power for a Roman one; but to take the place of the empire in Gaul, to succeed to its heritage, to reestablish its authority, under Frankish kings. Thus when the Empire of the West had ceased to be, the Frankish kings sought titles and alliances from the emperors who still ruled at Constantinople. It is a significant characteristic, indeed, of the Merwing monarchy that it kept up close relations with the distant Roman Empire in the East, that the Frankish kings professed to be the loyal allies, as they were often the formally adopted sons, of the Roman emperors and the consuls of the republic.

The Frankish kings, by their Christianity, imperfect though it was, were admitted to fellowship with the central power of the Christian world, with emperor at Byzantium and pope at Rome.

"Gaul was really independent of the empire in all

respects,"¹ and it is not there that we should seek for ecclesiastical relations with Constantinople. But there can be no question that the Catholicism of the Franks owed something to Eastern influences. There are points in the Gallican ritual which are distinctly Byzantine, and must belong to this period. Chlodowech, as an ally rather than a subject, and not least, perhaps, because he was a Catholic, received the dignity of the consulate from Anastasius.² And in the reign of the great Justinian the Merwings looked to the emperor for recognition and support. Theodebert, his "son," accepted a commission to propagate the Catholic faith in the imperial name.³ Bishops, too, who might be in need of advice and consolation, applied naturally to Constantinople. Nicetius, Bishop of Trier, that "man of highest sanctity, admirable in preaching, and renowned for good works,"⁴ persecuted by Chlothochar and his men, wrote naturally to the holy and orthodox emperor, "dominus semper suus." In the midst of barbarities scarce conceivable,⁵ the finest characters were trained by the simple verities of the Catholic faith, to which they clung with an extraordinary tenacity. Nor is this anywhere more strongly shown than in the history of the Franks. Of the meaning of the great struggle of Catholicism against Arianism, and of its immense personal value, the histories afford many instances. There is an eloquent passage in

¹ Bury, *History of the Later Roman Empire*, vol. i. p. 396.
² Greg. Tur., ii. 38 (Migne, *Patr. Lat.*, p. 236).
³ Bouquet, *Recueil*, tom. iv. p. 59, epist. 15: cf. Gasquet, *L'Empire byzantin et la Monarchie franque*, p. 165.
⁴ Greg. Turon., *Hist. Franc.*, x. 29 (Migne, p. 560): cf. also his *Vitae Patrum*, 17. Hontheim, *Historia diplomatica*, i. 47.
⁵ Cf. Greg. Turon., v. 3, on the frightful cruelty of Rauching.

Mr. Hodgkin's *Italy and her Invaders*,[1] which I cannot

The strength of the Catholic faith among the Franks. forbear to quote. "In the previous generation both Brunichildis and Galswintha had easily conformed to the Catholic faith of their affianced husbands. Probably the councillors of Leovigild expected that a mere child like Ingunthis would without difficulty make the converse change from Catholicism back into Arianism. This was ever the capital fault of the Arian statesmen, that, with all their religious bitterness, they could not comprehend that the profession of faith, which was hardly more than a fashion to most of themselves, was a matter of life and death to their Catholic rivals. Here, for instance, was their own princess, Brunichildis, reared in Arianism, converted to the orthodox creed, clinging to it tenaciously through all the perils and adversities of her own stormy career, and able to imbue the child-bride, her daughter, with such an unyielding devotion to the faith of Nicaea, that not one of all the formidable personages whom she met in her new husband's home could avail to move her by one hair's breadth towards 'the Arian pravity.'"

It was the strength of the Catholicism of those who were trained in it and by it, seen in Spain and Gaul as well as in Italy, which drew the Frankish churchmen naturally towards the great witnessing power of the Roman bishop. The pontificate of Gregory the Great affords significant illustrations of this influence.

From 595 the letters of S. Gregory show a continual interest in Gaul. A good deal of it is personal, concerned with the management of papal estates or with

[1] Vol. v. p. 252.

the relations of particular persons towards the pope himself. But Gregory was careful to assert a very special connection between Rome and the "lands of the Gauls" in all ecclesiastical matters. The Roman Church was the mother to whom they applied in time of need.[1] Gregory gave the pallium to Vergilius, bishop of the ancient city of Arles, and with it the position of papal vicar within the kingdoms of Burgundy, Austrasia, and Aquitaine. He recognised the terrible laxity of the Gallican Church : the clergy were negligent, simoniacal, vicious ; laymen were often consecrated to the episcopate. He gave counsel freely to the kings : Childebert he warmly commended : Brunichild, whose tenacious adherence to the Catholic faith he knew, while he probably knew but little of her personal character, he wrote to with paternal affection, granted the pallium at her request and that of Gallican bishops to S. Syagrius, Bishop of Autun, and appealed to her as one who had the will as well as the power to reform abuses, remove scandals, and destroy paganism. He set himself determinedly to work against the taint of money which hung over the whole Church. He earnestly pleaded for the expulsion of "these detestable evils," for the summoning of a synod which should reform the whole Church. He pleaded in vain ; but his work was not without lasting results. He founded the alliance between the papacy and the Frankish kings which was to be so fruitful in later history. And he founded it not with a political but with an entirely religious object. Through the court he hoped to reform the Church. He saw how closely Church and State were

Gregory the Great and Gaul.

[1] S. Greg., *Epp.* v. 58.

E

linked together, and he thought that he could make the kings act as rulers who set the Church's interest always first. It has been well said that his work, though the Church long remained corrupt, was not in vain. "He succeeded in establishing a regular intercourse between himself and the churches of Gaul, especially in the cities of the east and south; he fixed a tradition of friendship between the apostolic see and the Frank princes; he held up an ideal of Christianity before a savage and half-pagan people; and he caused the name of bishop to be once more reverenced in a land where it had grown to be almost synonymous with avarice, lawlessness, and corrupt ambition. If Gregory did no more than this he accomplished enough. Though his work was not rich in definite results at the moment, yet afterwards, in the reign of Charlemagne, its effects became manifest." [1]

At the same time the Frankish Church undoubtedly maintained a position distinctly independent of Rome.

Relations of the Frankish Church with Rome. Arles never really became a papal vicariate. Gregory's endeavours were fruitless in practical result.[2] The Gallican churches continued to be governed by their bishops, with every degree of local variety, not by the pope. Gregory rather set forth an ideal than established a subordination. His influence was personal not constitutional, and it was not strong. Yet in the days between Gregory and Charles the Great the links connecting Rome with Gaul were not weakened. Later on they were to be strengthened still more by the growth of a reformed monasticism, which gave support

[1] F. H. Dudden, *Gregory the Great*, ii. 69.
[2] Cf. E. Lavisse, *Hist. de France*, tome ii. p. 219.

to the papacy while yet it looked to the popes for
guidance. But meanwhile the influence of individual
ecclesiastics in Gaul must not be forgotten. As was so
often the case in medieval Europe, an age of wickedness presents, in the chronicles and biographics, a very
large proportion of lives which received the praise of
sanctity. Bishops, anchorites, monks, often, it would
seem, rose far above the standard of their day: men
noted their lives with awe and remembered them with
reverence. They moved in a society of curious com-
plexity.

Venantius Fortunatus, who dedicated his poems to
Gregory the Great, and was " the great man of letters
of his age, was a poet, but a Christian
poet—a writer of letters, but a close friend
of holy souls, and notably of S. Radegund,
the exiled princess and saint.¹ We learn
from him that even in those days of blood
there was a literary society at the Frankish courts,
and the savage king Chilperich made pretence to be a
writer, a theologian, and even a poet, though Gregory
of Tours assures us that he had not the least notion of
prosody.

Venantius Fortunatus and his literary friends,
Chilperich and his obsequious courtiers, link us to
another and more notable name. To one bishop, who
achieved canonisation, we owe very much of what we
know of the history of those times.

Gregory of Tours wrote memoirs which " are those
of a man who has played a great part in the State.
At the same time he has the sense for interesting

¹ M. Roger, L'Enseignement des lettres classiques d'Ausone à Alcuin,
p. 100.

things, miracles, and adventures, which is sometimes wanting in historians."[1]

We learn from his books that he had been trained in classic learning, and that the bishops of the day did not turn aside from the pagan classics. It is quite clear that his education was not merely theological or even exclusively Christian. Other writers he refers to, but with Vergil he certainly was familiar. And it is difficult to believe that he stood alone, bitterly though he complained of the ignorance of his contemporaries. The very fact that Gregory the Great denounced the custom of bishops studying and teaching classical grammar and classical fables, shows that the education of those days was not very closely confined. And of its results, seen also in a goodly list of clerical men of letters, Gregory of Tours is perhaps the best example.

Gregory of Tours.

He was before all things a bishop; he wrote indeed, as a French writer has happily said, "en évêque"; but he was also a statesman and a very keen observer of life. From his pages we learn how slight had been the impression that Christianity had yet made on the lives of barbarous men. We see kings still wondering that God's power could be greater than their own, yet when they were awoke to terror by the thought of death flying in craven fear to the feet of the minister of God. The whole history is a tale of treacheries and murders, of quarrels and of sins among men and women pledged to God; and yet it is evident that behind the cruelty and crime there was a new spirit at work, slowly transforming society by the conversion of individuals. It was a transforma-

[1] W. P. Ker, *The Dark Ages*, p. 125.

tion which was going on all over Europe; nowhere at this time, perhaps, more conspicuously than in Gaul and in Ireland. There are many parallels between the Celtic "age of saints" and the Merwing age of sinners. It is difficult to learn the full truth about either; but out of the darkness comes the conspicuous witness of individual saints. Of one or two of these a word may be said. Most notable is one who served both Ireland and Gaul.

The figure of the great Irish monk Columban is a light in the darkness of the gross and cruel Merwing age. Born about 540, he died in 615, after a life of achievement and hardness such as was given to few of his time. He died at Bobbio, crowned with the halo of heroism and sanctity ; but he was born in distant Ireland, and the main work of his life had been to introduce into Gaul the monastic movement which was led in Italy by S. Benedict. During the intellectual and moral weakness which the barbarian invasions brought upon the West the Church in Ireland appeared to stand forth resplendent in the security of her faith and virtue and in the cultivation of learning. In the warm Celtic nature the Gospel, so late introduced, had found a natural home. The monasteries which rose all over the land, with the huts of hermits and the cells of anchorites, were the seed-plots of religion and sacred lore. The community life of Christian religious was naturally grafted on to the old Druid stock. The tribes of the Goidels became the monasteries; the head of the family was the abbat; the country looked everywhere to the monks for leadership. Thus Armagh and Emly, Clonard, Ennismore, Clonfert, Clonmacnoise,

S. Colum-
ban (540-
615).

Bangor, arose to teach and govern the Church. Their monks lived by severe rule, based, no doubt, upon the customs of the East, of Egypt or Syria, most strict in the abasement of the selfish will, in penitence, in work, in prayer. "Good is the rule of Bangor," said the ancient sequence, "strait, austere, holy, and just." It was this rule, with the enthusiasm which marked all classes for religion and for knowledge, which inspired S. Columban in his great work. It was a work whose keynote was sacred study and which found its harmony in monastic service. S. Columban was the type, the representative *par excellence*, of the Irish monk, in his high idealism, his thirst for self-sacrifice, his adventurous and missionary spirit.

He was trained at Bangor, but there he could not stay. He was fired with the determination to spread the Gospel over sea, among the Gauls who, under a veneer of Christianity, still often lived a pagan life. There heathen superstitions still flourished, in worship of the old gods, in veneration of trees and rocks and idols: the heathen morals were hardly disguised. The Frankish society over which the Merwings ruled, the Gaul of Sigebert and Chilperich and Chlothochar, was stained with blood and lust. Apart from it altogether, it would seem, and exercising hardly any influence, were a few holy bishops and very many isolated monasteries, the homes of prayer and renunciation and penitence. In the sixth century it is said that some two hundred monasteries were founded in Gaul; but their protest against the vice of their age was for the most part a silent one. Columban, when he landed, was to make a more effective protest against the luxury of the time,

His work in Gaul.

the ineffective, unmeaning faith in the forgiveness of
sins apart from renunciation of them, which marked
the semi-Christian society into which he came.

Guntchramn, king of the Burgundians, gave him
a settlement at Annegray, and afterwards at Luxeuil,
where there grew up, on the site of an   Luxeuil
earlier Roman township, a monastery of   and its
stern and rigid rule. Eventually he added   rule.
a third foundation at Fontaine; and he presided over
three houses, governing according to a rule which he
himself drew up, after the examples of Clonard and
Bangor. Its characteristic was the completeness of
the self-denial aimed at; its motto the thought, "Think
not of what thou art, but of what thou shalt be";
its government an autocracy depending wholly on the
abbat; its scholarship not only that of the Bible, but
of the Latin classics—of Horace and of Vergil. Its
work was twofold. In the first place, it exemplified
a strict life of obedience, self-sacrifice, and prayer, the
home of which was ever ready to minister to sick
souls without; and, secondly, it supplied the religion
of the age with a penitential system—in the penitential based upon Irish models—which was of great
influence in the secular and ecclesiastical legislation of
the future. Columban was not favourably received by
all the episcopate of his new country. They were
men of different ideals, unacquainted with the culture
which meant so much to him; and their acceptance of
the general Western custom of observing Easter
caused a warm dispute with the Celtic monks. To
Gregory the Great and to the Gaulish bishops
Columban alike appealed on behalf of the custom he
had received; but finally, after more than thirty

years' residence in Burgundy, he consented to observe the Celtic custom in silence, without endeavour to make converts to it. A more grave enemy at the beginning of the seventh century was the wicked young Burgundian king, Theodoric, at whose court was his grandmother, Brunichild. His stern denunciations of vice, his refusal to recognise the king's unlawful children, brought on Columban the fury of the oppressor, and he was ordered away from Luxeuil into a sort of semi-captivity at Besançon, and thence into exile. Long he wandered through Gaulish lands, to Nevers, down the Loire to Nantes, whence it was said that the ship refused to bear him back to Ireland. At last, after a meeting with Chlothochar, King of Neustria, whose rule over all the Franks he had prophesied, he found refuge at Bregenz, by the lake of Constance. With him were several of his monks, among them the S. Gall whose settlement in those lands has given the name to a canton of what is now Switzerland. The long journey of the exiled monks, with their strange tonsure, their holiness, their alms, their works of healing, was a veritable mission. The journey eventually ended in Italy; the internecine strifes of the Merwings which ceased for the time in **Bobbio.** the union of the whole land of the Franks under Chlothochar, left Columban without interest in Gaul, and the Lombard sovereigns gave him a home at Bobbio, in the Apennines, where his monastery, aided by the holiness of Queen Theodelind, was a mighty influence in the conversion of Lombardy from Arianism. There, in 615, he died, the prophet of his age, the stern preacher of righteousness, the wise student, the faithful herdsman of souls.

Columban is a great figure, of the chief facts of whose life there is no doubt. It is not so with many others.

S. Patrick belongs, we do not doubt, to true history ; but there is no doubt as to the richness of the legendary element in his life. Much the same is true of S. Wandrille. Few Englishmen, we suspect, have heard his name; but he was a great figure in an age which Mabillon called golden in its religious aspect, the strange, wild time of the Merwings, the seventh century after Christ. In 648 S. Wandrille founded the abbey of Fontenelle, in the district of Caux. He lived till a great age, his death being probably much later than 667, to which year it has been assigned. His career affords a very vivid picture of the monastic life of the time, standing out amid the darkness of crime. He rightly emphasises the holiness and wisdom and learning of the great bishops of the Merwing age. It was their work as leaders, missionaries, statesmen in the highest Christian sense which the monasteries were called upon to continue and perfect. The monasteries were the refuge and the rallying-ground of those who fought against the secularisation of the Church at the hands of the Gallo-Roman aristocracy. S. Wandrille, born of the great Karling house, was a leader among leaders, statesman among statesmen, monk among monks. He was one who passed from a great though barbaric court, where he had been a trusted official, into the strictness of monastic training, and then into the solitude of secluded communion with God. Such lives as his were the great attractive forces of the seventh century ; such retreats as the valley of Fontenelle were the centres of Christian influence of the age.

Between these men and Gregory of Tours it might seem that there was little in common. But there were others whose lives combined the interests of the two, the interests of monk and statesman and bishop.

Another great clerk of the seventh century who must not be forgotten is S. Didier (Desiderius) of Cahors, at **S. Didier.** one time treasurer of Chlothochar II. and of Dagobert I., the friend of saints like Eloi (Eligius), Ouen, and Arnulf. Through him we learn something of the religious life of Southern Gaul. He died probably in 655, and thus he represented the earlier part of the seventh century. His biographer gives a long list of the holy bishops who were his contemporaries, and of the churches and monasteries which were scattered thickly over the land. The whole tone of his writing—earnest, biblical, spiritual, shows how the Church, in spite of weakness and sloth and failure in some of her chief men, yet held up a standard of right and justice, purity and devotion, which penetrated all over the country, into castles and humble homesteads, and profoundly affected the whole national life. And this work was concentrated in the public eye in those good men who at court, amid good and ill report, lived as servants of Him who went about doing good.

But while the Church was thus entering into all the national life, as a sharer in its interests of every kind, it was the monastic ideal, there can be little doubt, which ultimately exercised the greatest influence on the Franks. The saints who won reverence were for the most part monks. The work of Columban passed into the work of Benedict, and when Luxeuil accepted the Benedictine rule, and when the Council of Autun in 670 declared it to be the rule for all monks everywhere, a great step was taken towards the intimate union of Gaul with the rest of Christendom in the things on which they had begun to set most store.

CHAPTER V

THE PONTIFICATE OF GREGORY THE GREAT

ABOUT 540 was born in Rome, of a noble family, the great Pope Gregory, whose work was to place the papacy at the head of Italian politics, and to lay the lines on which papal action for many centuries was to be based. When he was a child it might well have seemed that Italy under a strong Gothic rule would submit to the Arian teaching which the State supported. Theodoric endeavoured to make an united Italy; but the Church knew that there could be no compromise on the doctrine of the perfect Godhead of the Lord Jesus, and her attitude preserved Italy both for Catholicism and for the Empire. Gregory was taught as a Catholic, but he was taught also in classical grammar, composition, rhetoric, and the writings of the great Romans—pre-Christian, as well as of later days. He began his life's work as a Roman official, and by the year 573 he is found as prefect of the city. A year later, it would seem, he became a monk, giving up all his property, all his signs of rank and wealth, all his power and place. Soon, if not at once, he came to serve under the rule of S. Benedict, whose life he afterwards wrote, in the monastery dedicated to S. Andrew on the Caelian hill.

Gregory the Great.

It was the time when Italy was again at the feet of the barbarians. The Lombards, the last of the Teutonic nations to settle in the West, established at Pavia a kingdom which lasted for two centuries (568-774), and which again rent away much of the fair Italian lands from the unity of the Empire, leaving the Exarchate at Ravenna in a state half isolated and wholly perilous.

The Lombard invasion, 568.

Gradually the onward sweep of the new barbarians, who called themselves Arians, but were not strongly bound by any creed, swept away all power save their own and the pope's. The destruction of Monte Cassino was typical of one side of their work—the turning aside from Rome at Gregory's intercession of another. The Empire struggled to retain its hold on Italy and to govern the Western world from Ravenna, with instructions from the New Rome; but it failed. The papacy studied to be quiet. And the close of the sixth century showed that power would return in the end to the city which had founded the Empire, and to the Church which was now claiming to teach and to unite the nations.

The effect on Italy.

A period of papal insignificance was gradually ended by the progress of new ideals for the papacy. This came about in three ways.

1. It was the aim of each pope to set up his power against that of the imperial exarchate, by which Italy was ruled after its reconquest by Belisarius and Narses. Gradually, step by step, the popes claimed cognisance of secular matters, intervened in politics, and stood forth as leaders in Italian affairs. The imperial administration saw the danger, and, from time to time, made definite

The popes and the exarchate.

opposition to the papal pretensions. It endeavoured
to restore the unity of the Church, to secure the
universal condemnation of the Three Chapters, but
under sanction of Ravenna rather than of Rome.
Thus the exarch Smaragdus, in 587, led Severus,
patriarch of Aquileia, before the Ravennate prelates
to make submission; [1] and later the emperor Maurice
interfered to prevent the pope compelling the patriarch
to submission. But these endeavours were futile; and
the great Gregory, statesman and administrator of the
first order, made the papacy the most important political power in the western provinces of the Empire. In
599 this was apparent in Gregory's negotiation with
the Lombard king, Agilulf.

2. The papal influence was increased, and the Greek
power diminished, by the direct replacement of Eastern
monks by Benedictines.[2] The monasteries
founded by Greeks during the imperial restoration, no longer replenished from Constantinople, fell into the hands of the great
papal force founded by the greatest saint, and mar-
shalled by the greatest administrator of the century.

The Bene-
dictines
in South
Italy.

3. And, lastly, the power of the papacy was at
once evidenced and increased by the revival of
its missionary energy. What Pelagius II.
had stayed, Gregory the Great accomplished
—the conversion of England by the mission
of Augustine. Spain, too, was won from Arianism
by a personal friend of Gregory's, though without
Roman intervention; [3] and within Italy itself the

Missions
from
Rome.

[1] *Paulus Diaconus*, iii. 26, ed. Waitz, pp. 105-7.

[2] Diehl, *op. cit.*, gives a list, p. 256.

[3] Joannes Biclarensis, *Chronicon* (Migne, *Patr. Lat.*, lxxii. 868).

pope began the great work of the conversion of the
Lombards to the Catholic faith, with the full teaching
both of the Tome of Leo and of the Fifth General
Council. Gregory sent the Acts of the Council to be
taught to the little child Adalwald, the Lombard king.

Thus in each of these three directions the progress of
papal power is connected with the influence of Gregory
the Great. It is of his papacy therefore that we must
speak as the critical point in the upward movement.
Between 574 and 590 Gregory gained experience in
many ways. To a strict monastic training he added, in
579, the employment of papal apocrisiarius (or envoy)
at the imperial court at Constantinople. Here he
became intimate with the chief ecclesiastics, with
Anastasius, who had been deposed from the patriarchal
see of Antioch, and who came to regard him as " the
very mouth and lantern of the Lord," with Leander of
Seville, who had come to lay the needs of the Catholic
cause in Spain before the emperors,[1] and with the
imperial family. About 586 he returned to
Rome, and became abbat of the monastery
in which he had formerly served. It was
there that he completed his commentary, or *moralia*,
on the book of Job, which he had delivered as lectures
at Constantinople, an epitome of Christian theology
and morals. It was then that he saw the bright lads
from Deira, who first turned his thoughts to the conversion of England.[2] The controversy of the Three
Chapters was still lingering on in Italy, and it was
Gregory who was given the task of inducing the Istrian

Gregory
as abbat.

[1] See below, p. 76.
[2] The *Vita Antiquissima* (S. Gall. MS), by a monk of Whitby,
does not represent them as slaves (pp. 13, 14), ed. Gasquet.

bishops to accept the decisions of the Fifth General
Gregory Council. So skilful did he prove himself
elected as a controversialist, as an administrator,
pope, 590. and as an adviser of Pelagius, that he was
elected with enthusiasm to succeed that pope in 590.

His ideal of the pastoral office is set forth in that
golden book, the *Liber regulae pastoralis*, in which he
The describes the life of a true shepherd of the
pastoral Christian people. A life of absolute purity
rule. and devotion as therein sketched was that
which made Gregory's pontificate notable for its
wisdom, its discretion, and its wise governance. The
pastoral office to him was one even more of the cure
of souls than of government, and that idea is shown in
all his letters. He wrote to kings, abbats, individual
Christians, with the spirit of direct encouragement and
admonition, as a wise teacher dispensing instruction.
In the Lateran he lived, as he had lived on the Caelian
hill, a life of strict ascetic rule, wearing still his monastic
dress, and living in common with his clerks and monks.
John the Deacon, who wrote his biography nearly two
centuries after his death, says that " the
Gregory's Roman Church in Gregory's time was like
life. that Church as it was under the rule of the
apostles, or the Church of Alexandria when S. Mark
was its bishop." Charity was by him developed into
a great scheme of benevolence organised with the
minutest care and recorded in detail in books that
were a model to later times. The political and ecclesiastical cares of the papacy never prevented Gregory
from what he considered the chiefest duty of his
office, that of preaching. His sermons, which were as
famous as those of Chrysostom in Constantinople, were

direct in their appeal, vivid in their illustration, terse and epigrammatic in their expression. Paul the Deacon sums up his work by saying that he was entirely engrossed in gaining souls.

At the same time he was a statesman as well as a bishop. He governed the "patrimony of S. Peter," lands scattered over Italy and even Gaul, with a careful supervision, entering into minute matters as well as general policy, freeing slaves, caring for the cultivation of land; and the intimate knowledge which he thus acquired is shown in his *Dialogues*, which throw a flood of light on the life, secular as well as ecclesiastical, of his age. Outside these districts, in purely spiritual matters, he showed a constant vigilance. Everywhere what was needed seemed to be known to the pope, and everywhere he was planning to remedy evils, to build up the Church, to reform abuses, to convert heretics, to supply new bishops, to encourage the growth of monasticism. This activity extended not only to what were called the suburbicarian provinces but to distant lands, such as Spain, Illyricum, Gaul, Africa, as well as to Northern Italy. Something has been said of his relations in Gaul, and remains to be said of his intervention in Africa. His relations with Constantinople may be most significantly illustrated by the dispute as to the title of the patriarch of New Rome.

In 588 the acts of a synod of Constantinople were declared by Pelagius II. to be invalid because the patriarch used the title οἰκουμεν- ικός or *universalis*. Just as at the Council of Chalcedon the Alexandrine representatives styled the pope "œcumenical archbishop and pat-

His states-manship

The title "Uni-versal Bishop"

F

riarch of the Great Rome," so the patriarch of Constantinople used the style and dignity of "œcumenical
patriarch." It was one that had been employed at
least since 518, and it seems to have been commonly
used. From the use of this title came grave controversy. In 588 the acts of a synod of Constantinople were declared by Pelagius II. to be invalid
because the patriarch used the title οἰκουμενικός or
universalis: and in 595 Gregory the Great strongly
condemned the use of such a phrase, at the same time
repudiating its use for his own see. "The Council
of Chalcedon," he wrote, " offered the title of *universal*
to the Roman pontiff, but he refused to accept it, lest
he should seem thereby to derogate from the honour
of his brother bishops."[1] And to the emperor Maurice
he said still more distinctly, " I confidently affirm that
whosoever calls himself *sacerdos universalis,* or desires
to be so called by others, is in his pride a forerunner
of Antichrist." But the patriarchs continued to use
the title, and before a century had elapsed, the popes
followed their example.

The relation of Gregory with the Church of
Illyricum gives opportunity for mention of that
anomalous patriarchate. Somewhat apart
from the general Church history of the
early Middle Age stands the province of
Illyricum. Its ecclesiastical status was even more
ambiguous than its political. On its borders, or within
its limits, the patriarchate of Rome touched that of

The pro-
vince of
Illyricum.

---

[1] S. Greg., *Epp.*, v. 18. The term *sacerdos* is commonly used for
bishop at this date. Thus Gregory of Tours calls a bishop *sacerdos*
during this life, *antistes* after his death. S. Gregory must not, however, be understood as disclaiming a papal supremacy.

THE PONTIFICATE OF GREGORY

Constantinople, and the claims of the two, sometimes
at least conflicting, were complicated by the privileges
given by Justinian to his birthplace. In the tenth
century it was undoubtedly under the jurisdiction of
Constantinople, in the seventh it appears to have been
under that of Rome. In the Councils at Constantinople in 681 and 692, the Illyrian bishops appeared
as attached exclusively to Rome; and so, it has been
noticed, did those of Crete, Thessalonica, and Corinth.
In the sixth century there are instances, though not
numerous ones, of papal interference, in the nature of
the exercise of judicial power, in the province of Illyricum; and at the end of the century Gregory the
Great was especially active in his correspondence with
the bishops. It would seem from one of his letters
that he counted even Justiniana Prima as under his
authority, though the intention of the emperor was
certainly not to make it so. This edict—for so it
practically is—is interesting also because it appears
to deal with all the ecclesiastical provinces of the
empire which depended immediately on the Roman
patriarchate. It omits Africa, and the fact that the
popes did not send the pallium to the Bishop of
Carthage (the North African Metropolitan) shows
that the popes did not claim to confer jurisdiction,
but merely to recognise a special relationship, by this
act.[1] On the other hand, it is to be observed that the
code of Justinian contains a law of Theodosius II.
which places the Illyrian bishopric under the jurisdiction of the patriarch of Constantinople. But this
law is beset with many difficulties, and it has been

[1] The letter is Epp. Greg. (Jaffé), 1497 ; cf. letter to Syagrius,
Bishop of Autun.

argued that it was merely the expression of a temporary rupture between the Empire and the papacy, which in the schism of 484–519 was gravely accentuated; and there are grounds for thinking that the bishops of Thessalonica exercised authority in Illyricum as delegates of Rome—yet rather from their political than their ecclesiastical associations. However this may be, there can be no doubt that the position given by Justinian to the city of his birth was intended to be practically patriarchal, and that the Bishop of Thessalonica, whether vicar or not of the pope, was practically ignored. The whole question is indeed a notable example of the difficulties consequent on the close connection between religion and politics in the sixth century.

Gregory's action was that of a wise but masterful ruler, and it seems to have been based on the view

Gregory's claim to jurisdiction.

that all the bishops of the West were directly under his jurisdiction. Similar cases of interference are to be found in regard to the churches of Istria, and to the great sees of Ravenna and Milan. In connection may be seen the claim to grant the *pallium*, a mark of honour which seems to have been gradually passing into a sign of jurisdiction.[1] Gregory claimed for the successors of S. Peter something like an apostolic authority, and he at least suggested a theory of the papal office which was capable of almost indefinite extension. Politics and religion here met together. When Airulf in 592 appeared before Rome the pope made a separate treaty with him: he stepped into the

[1] It does not seem, from Bede i. 39, that, as has been asserted, it was always necessary to apply for it.

place of ruler of imperial Italy when he disregarded
the exarch and even the emperor, and entered into
negotiations on his own account; and up to the time
of his death he was practically responsible for the re-
arrangement of Italy. His letter to the great Lombard queen, Theodelind, of whom memorials survive
to-day at Monza, show how the two sides of his
position mingled; how he was statesman and diplo-
matist as well as priest and missionary.

In his missionary interests he passed far outside
Italy. The most conspicuous example is the conversion
of the English, which he had in earlier
years been most anxious himself to under-   His
take, and which was begun in 597 under   missions.
his direction by Augustine; but it is not the only one.
In Northern Italy, in Africa and Gaul, Gregory was
active in seeking the conversion of pagans and heretics,
and in endeavouring by gentle measures to lead the
Jews to Christ.

More important still in the history of the papacy
was Gregory's work in spreading, organising, and
systematising monasticism. He insisted on   His
the strict observance of the rule of S.   relations to
Benedict. Not only did he reform, but he   monasti-
very greatly strengthened, the monasticism   cism.
of Italy. Conspicuously did his *privilegia*, granting or
recognising a considerable freedom from episcopal
control, start the monks on a new advance. While
not exempting them from the rule of bishops, he made
it possible for future popes to win support for themselves by granting such exemptions.

But Gregory's fame does not lie wholly in any
of these spheres of activity. Great as a ruler and an

organiser, he was known also to later ages, as to his own, for his theological writings. He was not only a practical ruler and practical minister of Christ; he was also a leader in Christian learning—the last, as men have come to call him, of the four great Latin doctors.

The work of Gregory the Great was here as elsewhere far - reaching, but rather an organising **His relations to learning.** than a formative one. Classical studies, in which he had been trained, he put aside; and when he did his utmost to spread monasteries over the length and breadth of Italy, it was not at all of learning in a secular sense, but wholly of religion that he thought. Thus his own theology is primarily a biblical theology. The Bible was to him the word of God. Like the author of the *Imitatio Christi* in later days, he did not care to argue as to the authorship of the different books but to profit by what was in them. He was a great expositor, a great preacher, and that always with **His doctrine of the Church.** a practical aim. As he said, "We hear the words of God if we act on them." In his more general theological writings he sums up, with the precision of a master, not any new doctrines or advances in speculation, but the theology of the Church of his age. And he is able thus to emphasise the crying need of unity in words which state the claim of the Church for the conversion of the pagans and heretics of his day: "Sancta autem universalis ecclesia prædicat Deum veraciter nisi intra se coli non posse, asserens quod omnes qui extra ipsam sunt minime salvabuntur." Outside this there was no hope of spiritual health. And this doctrine he based

on the unity of Christ's life with that of the Church:
"Our Redeemer showed that He is one person with
the Church, which He took to be His own"; and thus
it was that "The Churches of the true faith set in all
parts of the world make one Catholic Church, in which
all the faithful who are right minded toward God live
in concord." Thus he was, in theology as in ecclesiastical politics, a concentrating and clarifying force; and
when, on March 12th, 604, he passed to his rest, he
had laid firm the foundations of the medieval papacy,
and in hardly less degree those of the theological system of the medieval Church.

CHAPTER VI

CONTROVERSY AND THE CATHOLICISM
OF SPAIN

CONTROVERSIES which belong to this period are those connected with semi-Pelagianism and with Adoptianism. Faustus, Bishop of Riez, who died almost at the end of the fifth century, held views which were **Pelagian controversy of the sixth century.** opposed to those of S. Augustine as well as to those of Pelagius. His writings were attacked by many, among them by Caesarius, Bishop of Arles from 501 to 542, who caused a synod at Orange in 529 to condemn semi-Pelagian opinions, in a statement which declared that sufficient grace is given to all the baptized (an expression which had an important history centuries later). The writings of Faustus were the subject of much discussion also at Constantinople, and they were condemned by several of the popes.

Of a wholly different kind was the heresy originating in the East, and probably revived through the controversy of the Three Chapters, which came into prominence in the eighth century in Spain. It has been thought that the exigencies of anti-Muhammadan controversy had something to do with the importance which the question now assumed. The Spanish Church had a long record, in the Councils of Toledo, of orthodox and

THE CATHOLICISM OF SPAIN

strenuous adherence to the Christian faith; but it
showed also a strongly nationalistic spirit, and it was
natural that much should be developed, through an-
tagonism to Muhammadanism and Arian influences,
which would fall into danger of extreme reaction on
the one side or of unwise concession on the other.
" Spanish Christianity," it has been said in a phrase
which has become classical, "was a perpetual crusade."
In Spain the Christian contest against sin and un-
belief became more often, or more constantly, than
elsewhere an actual physical struggle against those
who distorted or denied the faith of the Church and
those who trampled it under foot. This is, of course,
most true of the ages which followed the Moorish
invasions, of the long strife between Christians and
Moors, of the times and the thoughts which gave
birth to the immortal literature of the peninsula, to
Calderón and Cervantes, to Lope de Vega and S.
Teresa of Jesus. But it is also true, though in a less
degree, of the earlier times—of those which extended
from the introduction of Christianity—from the missionary visit, it may be, of S. Paul himself—down to
the destruction of the monarchy of the Wisigoths in
711. Spain was in 589 won to Catholicism by the
conversion of its king Reccared. But this was the end
of a long and critical period, for from the acceptance
of Arianism by Remismond in 466 the country was
under the rule of princes who were pledged to that
error.

The Wisigoths identified their heresy with their
nationality. The general decadence of the Empire
spread to Spain. The social system was in a state of
dissolution. The canons of the Councils show a pic-

ture of life which is appalling in its corruption, but
at the same time are evidence of the earnest efforts
of the Church for amendment. They show how Christianity had penetrated into the country districts, and
how eager were the bishops of the sixth century to
do their spiritual duty far and wide. Side by side
with the canons of Church Councils is the great
Fuero Jusgo (in process of compilation from the fifth
to the eighth century) in witnessing to the efforts
for a better state of things. During the rule of the
The con-   West Goths, persecution of Catholics had
version of been frequent, but when Amalric married
Spain.   Hlothild, daughter of Chlodowech, promis-
ing her tolerance of her religion, a way was opened
for a new life to orthodoxy. But Amalric broke his
promise, and an invasion of Spain by the Franks followed. In the reign of the Arian Theudis (531–48)
there was still more decisive intervention. Childebert
and Chlothochar invaded Spain and besieged Saragossa,
but were driven back; and it was not till Athanagild
called in the armies of Justinian that the confusion
and division of Spanish life, between orthodox and
heretic, Roman and Goth, was healed in the slightest
degree. The year 560 witnessed the conversion of
King Mir by Martin of Braga, and three years later,
and again in 572, Councils at Braga witnessed to the
Catholic faith of the Church. But it was an era of
fightings and fears. The Roman armies of the Eastern
Empire held the cities of the coast long after Athanagild had come to be recognised as king of all the Goths
in Spain, but gradually unity was springing up under
the rule of that able chieftain. He died in 568, having
married his daughters, Brunichild and Galswintha, to

THE CATHOLICISM OF SPAIN 75

the Frankish kings, Sigebert and Chilperich. His successor Leovigild established a sway over all the Visigothic possessions and ruled from Nîmes to Seville. The wedding of Brunichild, though sung by Venantius Fortunatus, Bishop of Poitiers, was but the beginning of crime and of sorrows; yet it led indirectly to the conversion of Spain. Brunichild's daughter Ingunthis married Leovigild's son Hermenigild. She was bitterly persecuted as a Catholic when she came to Spain, but she clung to her faith with the devotion of a martyr, and she won over her husband.

Hermenigild.

At Seville Hermenigild was for some time acting as king, under his father, and when he was threatened on his conversion with the loss of all he had he took up arms. After a long contest he was subdued, and he underwent a long persecution ending eventually in death when he refused to receive communion at the hands of an Arian bishop on Easter Day, 585.[1] Ingunthis escaped to Constantinople. Then till 587 Arianism reigned supreme in Spain, and John of Biclaro, Catholic bishop of Gerona, writes as one crying in a wilderness. But Catholicism in Spain was scotched, not killed, and when Reccared (586–601) called Arian and Catholic bishop alike before him, and after two years definitely accepted orthodoxy under the influence of his uncle Leander, Archbishop of Seville, it was not long before the whole of Spain accepted his decision and followed his example. This was in 587, and an inscrip-

Council of Toledo, 589.

[1] This story is discredited by a recent writer, Mr. Dudden, S. Gregory the Great, i. 407 (following F. Görres), but I see no reason to doubt that S. Gregory was rightly informed, and I accept what Dr. Hodgkin (Eng. Hist. Rev., ii. 216) states as the facts.

tion shows that the cathedral church of Toledo was then consecrated in the Catholic faith. With the Council of Toledo (third synod of Toledo), 589,[1] which accepted the first four General Councils and the Procession of the Holy Ghost from the Father and the Son, Spain returned to the unity of the faith. From Reccared's reign, too, dates a civilisation distinctly traceable to Constantinople and a recognition of absolute equality between the different races in the peninsula. And to that golden age belong also the great saint and preacher, Leander, who died in 603, and S. Isidore of Seville, the encyclopædic writer, who died thirty-three years later. S. Leander had at Constantinople come to know Gregory the Great. He was the chief theologian of Spain in his age, and his words welcomed and ratified the conversion. Thus the modern history of Spain and her most Catholic kings begins. The importance of the period culminates in the compilation, almost final, of the great Wisigothic Code, the Fuero Jusgo, at once civil and ecclesiastical, the result of a union between Church and State even more perfect than that represented in the English Witenagemot.

The concentration of Spanish interests on theological questions led before long to new developments, but meanwhile it helped the happy tendency to unity which Recceswinth (652-72) confirmed by allowing the intermarriage which had long been forbidden—Recceswinth, whose splendid gold crown, dedicated to the Blessed Virgin, still remains amongst the most striking memorials of the Christian art of the seventh century. Wamba, his successor, established his supremacy in

[1] Mansi, *Concilia*, ix. 977–1010.

Septimania by the capture of Nîmes from a traitorous
vicegerent, and lived to show the sincerity with which
the Wisigoths had accepted the idea of the sanctity of
vows to God. During an illness, when he was supposed
to be incapable of recovery and remained in a stupor,
he received the tonsure that he might die as a monk:
when he recovered he refused to return to the world
and abdicated the throne. His successors were equally
strict, it would seem, in obedience to the Church's
laws, often unintelligently interpreted.

To these days, too, belongs one of the first and darkest blots on the popular Christianity of the Middle
Age—the persecution of Jews. The Jews of Spain   Persecu-
had long been restless under a government   tion of
which was so strongly ecclesiastical in its   the Jews.
sympathies: persecuting laws oppressed
them, and they could hardly even in secret practise
their religion. Plots were constant and natural, and
at last it is said that the Jews incited the Saracens,
who had overthrown the imperial power in Africa, to
cross the sea and strip from the weak Wisigoths of
Spain the last remains of their power. In 695 a
Council at Toledo (the sixteenth) determined when
the plot was discovered wholly to destroy the Judaic
faith in their land. It was ordered that all grown-up
Jews should be made slaves, and all children brought
up as Christians. This was the very year   Invasion
of the storming of Carthage.[1] It is not to   of the
be wondered at that the Jews gave every   Muham-
help they could to the infidels who, before   madans.
long, attacked the kingdom of the Wisigoths. Within
twenty years Spain, up to the very mountains of the

[1] See below, p. 109.

Basque land and of the Asturias, was conquered by
the followers of Muhammad, and silence fell upon
the country which had appeared to be the home of an
abiding Church.

The splendid edifice which had seemed to be reared
on the solid foundations of religion and law was
shattered by the repeated blows of the Arab invasion.
Why was this ? The chroniclers gave answer without
hesitation—" Peccatis exigentibus, victi sunt Chris-
tiani." The Goths (as they proudly called themselves)
" have so offended Thee, O Lord, by their pride, that
they deserved a fall by the sword of the Saracen."
It was, in truth, as the great Sancho of Navarre
declared in his charter of foundation to the abbey of
Albelda, " Our ancestors sinned without scruple ; they
daily transgressed the commandments of the Lord,
and so to punish them as they had deserved and to
make them turn to Him, the Most Just of Judges
delivered them to a barbarous people." In truth, the
mass of the land had never been converted to Catholic
Christianity at all, and a heretical society was power-
less against Moslem sincerity and swords. Only in
the north was Catholicism supreme, and thence came
in later days the reconquest. But Catholics lived on
all over Spain under their conquerors in comparative
peace.

The Church survived. Persecution made its life
strong and vigorous, and that life found outlet in new

The
Adoptian-
ist heresy.
varieties of theological expression. Elipandus, Archbishop of Toledo, within seventy
years of the Saracen conquest, became known
outside his own land, with Felix, bishop of the northern
see of Urgel, for his advocacy of the statement that

Christ's Sonship was that of adoption. Asserting the two Natures and the two Wills of the Lord, the Adoptianists regarded Christ as only in His divine nature truly the Son of God. Eager to assert the full Humanity and to rebut the Muhammadan charges of idolatry, the Spanish theologians taught that " one and the same Person was in two aspects a Son, in virtue of His relation to two different natures," and that " the Divine Son of God, begotten from all eternity of the Father, not by adoption but by birth, not by grace but by nature—that He, when made of a woman, made under the law, was Son of God, not by origin but by adoption, not by nature but by grace." [1] It was an attempt to carry further the decisions adopted at Chalcedon and to account for the origin of the two Natures, their completeness in distinction, and their union together.

Adoptianism was condemned at Regensburg in 792, and at Frankfort in 794, and, under the influence of Alcuin, Felix made submission at Aachen in 799. Elipandus, safe among the Saracens, held out in his opinions. It would seem that the discussion represented the eighth-century expression of the age-long conflict between logic and mystery, the desire for exact definition, and the sense of something beyond human understanding in what belongs to the nature of God, and to the divine action in the Incarnation, the union of God and man.

Adoptianism had in the East a greater success and a longer history than in the West. In Syria and Armenia vast numbers joined the sect founded, or revived, by one Con-

Its condemnation.

Adoptianism in the East.

[1] See R. L. Ottley, Doctrine of the Incarnation, ii. 152-4.

stantine in the middle of the seventh century. He lived near Samosata, and probably inherited the teaching of the earlier heretic, Paul of that place. The sect came to be called Paulicians. They rejected the real divinity of Christ and placed themselves in opposition to very much else which belonged to the earliest Christian tradition, as in their rejection of the Old Testament and the perpetual virginity of the Lord's Mother. Armenia became the headquarters of a large and prosperous sect, towards which emperors alternately were persecuting or favourable. Nicephorus I. (802–11) was friendly to it, but his successor put it down with relentless savagery; and after it had led to a formidable rebellion, its votaries were finally suppressed by the generals of Basil the Macedonian, 871. But its tenets lingered on in Thrace, whither it had been transported when some of its disciples were expropriated by Constantine V., till the eighteenth century, and still later in Armenia itself. The authoritative book of the Armenian Paulicians, the *Key of Truth*, has been thought to have been completed by one Smbat, minister of Chosroes of Persia, whose date is 800–50,[1] but the history of those days is certainly very confused and may have been distorted.

The intervention of Charles the Great in this controversy is but one illustration of the importance of theological questions in the outlook of the reviver of the Empire in the Catholic West. Other theological doctrines had a like interest in his view and in that of his house; and in some of them also Spain was concerned. At Toledo, in 589, Reccared, when he accepted the Catholic creed, had inserted his belief in

[1] See F. C. Conybeare, *The Key of Truth*, p. 67.

the double procession of the Holy Ghost. This was again discussed in 767 at Gentilly, and at Aachen in 809.

Alcuin, as in the Adoptianist controversy, played a great part in stating the view which the West was coming generally to accept. Leo III. was consulted, and advised that no addition should be made to the Creed for fear of widening the breach with the East. It would seem that the great hymn, " Veni Creator Spiritus," is the expression of this doctrine by the ninth century, and is the work of Rabanus Maurus, a monk of the famous house of Fulda.

The "Veni Creator."

While this sums up in devotional form the Christian thought as to one of the mysteries of faith, the hymn of a character more distinctly credal, called " Quicunque vult," enshrines it in another aspect. The " Quicunque " has, indeed, a much earlier history. In 633 the Fourth Council of Toledo quoted many of its clauses. Leod-gar, Bishop of Autun (663–78), directed his clergy to learn it by heart; and it became a not uncommon profession of faith to be made by a bishop at his consecration. At the end of the eighth century it seems to have been widely recited in church. But it certainly goes back very much earlier. Caesarius, Bishop of Arles (501–43), the opponent of semi-Pela-gianism, has been proved to have used the creed continually : it was quoted also by his rival, Avitus, Bishop of Vienne (490–523), and it is probable that it represents the teaching of the great abbey of Lerins in the controversies of the beginning of the sixth century. It was decisively a Western creed : it

The "Quicunque Vult."

G

never came into the offices of the orthodox Church
of the East. In the West it became a popular means
of instruction and a popular confession of the joy
of Christian faith. It was sung in procession, recited
in the services, meditated on by the clergy. It formed
a model of orthodox expression of belief in days of
confusion and controversy.

CHAPTER VII

THE CHURCH AND THE MONOTHELITE
CONTROVERSY, 628-725

THE years of peace that succeeded the death of
Justinian ended with the triumph of the Empire
over barbarian foes. Christian philosophy had seemed
to be quiescent, but there were questions which
thoughtful men must have seen would soon come up
for solution as the inevitable result of the Monophysite controversy. Thought in the active Eastern minds
could not stand still; and the West too, as the barbarians were conquered, assimilated, and converted by
the Church, began to enter keenly into the theology of
the East. In Gaul and Britain, as well as at Milan
and at Rome, there arose critics and historians who
could carry on the work of Leo the Great and of the
line of chroniclers who had told in Greek the story of
the Church's life. A word at first as to the general
interest of the period.

With the victory of Heraclius over the Persians in
628, it might seem that heresy would be driven from
its home in the distant East, that Nestor- The East
ianism would die out, and that Sergius I., in the
Patriarch of Constantinople (610-38), would seventh
be able to win back the Monophysites to century.
the unity of the Church. But this happy result was

83

prevented by the spread of the Muhammadan conquest, beginning even before the death of the Prophet in 632, and by the rise of a new heresy—the Monothelitism which gave to the two Natures of our Lord but a single will. As the Mussulman arms spread the faith of Islam, the Jacobite Church of Syria seemed almost to welcome it as a refuge from the dominance of orthodoxy. In Egypt the Coptic (Monophysite) patriarch entered Alexandria in triumph with the Muslim force when the Orthodox patriarch fled with the imperial troops. The Melkite (Orthodox) body was, however, not wholly unprotected by the conquerors, and at Jerusalem it was allowed to remain in possession, though at Antioch there was for long no Orthodox patriarch at all. Of the Monothelite heresy—condemned at the Sixth General Council, 681—we may for the moment defer to speak, except to note that in the political disturbances that swept over the Lebanon the heresy took root there, under one John Maron, and founded the division, religious and political, of the Maronites, which still endures.

But while the Church was thus suffering in various ways, the Byzantine missionary energy was far from exhausted. Heraclius sought to convert the barbarian tribes far and near, the Croats and Serbs, the Bulgarians and Slavs, and the Church of Constantinople appointed an official to inspect the districts on the frontiers and to examine candidates for baptism. Equally he sought to reunite the Armenians to the Orthodox Church; but after interviews and theological discussions the opponents of the Greeks triumphed, and the catholicos Nerses

Missionary work.

III. in 645 anathematised the Council of Chalcedon— a declaration which, after a momentary reunion, was renewed early in the eighth century. The Armenian Church thus remained formally Monophysite. While the orthodox emperors were thus unsuccessful in re-uniting the separated Churches, the patriarchate of Constantinople was winning a strength within which she had lost without; the area of her confined jurisdiction was straitly ruled, and 356 bishoprics towards the end of the seventh century acknowledged the patri-archal throne. The emperors and the Church alike recognised no supremacy of Rome—a fact which was emphasised by the decree of 666 which declared Ravenna free from papal jurisdiction, and in the con-demnation of Honorius by the Sixth General Council. So, again, the Council at Constantinople called *in Trullo* (691), directed canon after canon against the customs and claims of the Roman Church. The This independence was emphasised by the Trullian compilation of a *Syntagma*, or collection of Council, canons, parallel to the much later collec- 691. tion in the West. These canons, it may be remarked in passing, throw most interesting light on the customs of the Greek Church—on clerical marriage, for ex-ample, which was allowed to be dissolved only by the clergy of the recently converted barbarous tribes, among whom a return to celibate life might sometimes be advisable.

So much for the general characteristics of the period 628-725. We may now turn to the critical point of theology on which the ecclesiastical history of the time turned.

Monophysitism was not dead in spite of Chalcedon

or Constantinople. The Fourth and Fifth General
The   Council had still left points of debate for
Aphtharto-   those within as well as those without the
docetic con- Church. In the form which it was asserted
troversy.   that Justinian had himself come to accept,
it asserted the Lord's Body to be incapable of sin or
corruption, and only subject to suffering by the
voluntary exercise of His divine power. While the
accusations against Justinian in John of Nikiu and
Nicetius of Trier are contradictory to each other, and
make it clear that he did not accept the opinion of
Julian of Halicarnassus, they may serve to illustrate
the confusion of thought with which these subjects
were handled. The followers of Julian, whose view has
here been summarised, were nicknamed by those of
the famous monk Severus (Monophysite patriarch of
Antioch in 513), "Aphthartodocetes" or "Phantasiasts."
Those who followed Severus, while they were prepared
to recognise two natures in Christ, yet dwelt strongly
on their union, and especially on the "one energy"
of the Lord's will. From this a further step was to
be taken. There were some who believed in the transformation of the human nature into the Divine, and
who came to be called *Aktistetes*, and, in a still further
extreme, *Adiaphorites*, when they denied any distinction between the Godhead and manhood in Christ.
The error at the root of all these contentions seems to
have been the dwelling upon the physical rather than
the spiritual effects of the Divine power revealed in
the incarnation of the Son of God. Theologians arose
to controvert it and to develop the theological
decisions of the Council; chief among them was
Leontius of Byzantium, a philosophic apologist of real

eminence, whose work was taken up later and completed by John of Damascus.

It is not to be wondered at that a great soldier, filled
with a deep sense of the necessity of uniting the
Empire against its foes, should be led to   The
accept a theological development which   Emperor
seemed to offer the hope of a reconciliation. Heraclius
From 622, under the advice of Sergius,   as a
Patriarch of Constantinople, a basis of re-   theologian.
union was sought in the formula that though the Lord
had two Natures He had yet only "one theandric
energy." The emperor Heraclius turned unwisely
from the army to the Church, which, like many able
military men, he thought might be coerced or led into
opinions which seemed to him to be common sense.
For a time it appeared that he would succeed : three
patriarchs of Constantinople, one of Antioch, one of
Alexandria, one of Rome (Honorius I.), were in agreement, if a little tepidly, favourable to the phrase.
Honorius definitely stated that he confessed " one WILL
of our Lord Jesus Christ."[1] Only Sophronius, Patriarch
of Jerusalem (634), held out. In 638 the emperor
issued the Ecthesis,[2] or Confession of Faith, drawn up
by the patriarch Sergius. It professed ad- The
herence to orthodox definitions, and con- Ecthesis,
tinued, "Wherefore, following the Holy   638.
Fathers in all things, and in this, we confess one
Will of our Lord Jesus Christ, the very God, so that
never was there a separate Will of His Body animated

---

[1] This is spoken of by a recent Roman Catholic writer as "la
déplorable réponse de Honorius, ce monument de bonne foi surprise
et de naïveté confiante." It does not support the notion of papal in-
fallibility   [2] Given in Baronius, A.D. 639.

by the intellect, nor one of contrary motion natural to itself, but one which operated when and how and to what purpose He who is God the Word willed." This statement was repudiated by Rome, and in 649 condemned in a synod at the Lateran under Martin I., who ended his days in exile for disobeying the imperial power. The quarrel became one between Rome and Constantinople, at a time when the popes had recovered their orthodoxy and the patriarchs were subservient to impetuous emperors. In 648 the *Type* issued from

The Type, 648.

New Rome as an attempt at pacification; but the Old Rome rejected it, with anathemas.

In 680 a synod, under Pope Agatho, at which S. Wilfrith of Ripon was present and signed for the north part of Britain, rejected as heresy the doctrine of the two wills, and local councils (as at Hatfield six months later) agreed with the rejection.

Sixth General Council, 681.

All this led on to the summoning of the Sixth General Council at Constantinople, which sat from November, 680, to September, 681. The temporary schism between Rome and Constantinople was healed. Agatho's letter condemning the doctrine of the two wills was accepted; anathema was laid upon those, dead or alive, who had accepted the heresy, and among them Pope Honorius I., a condemnation repeated by many a pope after him. The Council declared that the Lord possesses two wills, " for just as the Flesh is, and is said to be, the Flesh of the Word, so also His human will is, and is said to be, proper [natural] to the Word." And also, " just as His holy and spotless ensouled flesh was taken into God yet not annihilated, so His human will though taken into God was not annihilated." Again, as so often in

the days of Justinian, the words of S. Leo were appro-
priated for a definition of the orthodox belief. The
Council was attended by 289 bishops, the emperor
occupying the position which had been common since
Nicaea, while on his right were the bishops of the East,
on his left those of the West. Rightly was the
doctrine of one will condemned as contrary to the
Chalcedonian assertion of the Lord's perfect Humanity;
and the condemnation was readily accepted by the
Church. Only in Syria, among the Maronites (followers of John Maro), did Monothelitism linger on for
centuries, till they became absorbed in the Latin
Church.

The chief opponent of Monothelitism was Maximus,
whose *Disputation with Pyrrhus* remains the most important survival of the controversy. It is **The Monothe-**
a subtle and rational exposition of the ortho- **Monothe-**
dox doctrine. The original phrase, *theandric* **lite**
energy, from which the Ecthesis of Heraclius **contro-**
started, seems to have been drawn from the **versy.**
unknown Platonist who came to be called Dionysius
the Areopagite, and whose writings had a continued
influence in the Middle Age. But to all reasonable
thinkers the main question was decided. The truth
of Christ's human nature was an essential verity of
the faith, and to deny His human will would make
His nature incomplete, and His goodness in any true
sense impossible. The difficulty would arise again
when Luther and Calvin carried further the dispute
concerning the nature of the human will, but as
regards her Lord the Church had come to a decision
based upon her knowledge of His divine life on earth.
The Council *in Trullo* (named from the dome-

shaped place of meeting), 691, called also *Quini-sextan*, summoned by Justinian II. (685–711), was not Œcumenical, and was disciplinary rather than dogmatic. It condemned many Roman practices, and asserted definitely that the patriarchal throne of Constantinople should enjoy the same privileges as that of Old Rome, should in all ecclesiastical matters be entitled to the same pre-eminence, and should rank as second after it. The *Liber Pontificalis*, the Roman Church history of the time, states that the pope's legates gave assent to the decrees, which is unlikely. But this one was no more than the repetition of many previous statements, as emphatic in the sixth as in the seventh century. The position was simply that claimed by the patriarch John when he signed the formula of Catholic faith drawn up and proposed by Pope Hormisdas. He insisted on prefixing a repudiation of the Roman claim to supremacy over Christendom. "I hold," he declared, "the most holy Churches of the Elder and the New Rome to be one. I define the See of the Apostle Peter and this of the Imperial City to be one See." By this it is clear that he designed to assert both the unity of the Church—which, as it has always seemed to the East, was threatened by the demand of the Roman obedience—and the equality of the two great churches of the Old and the New Rome.

Repudiation of Roman claims.

Justinian I. spoke of Constantinople as "head of all the churches" ("omnium ecclesiarum caput"), but it is clear that he did not regard this position as conferring any supreme or exclusive jurisdiction. It was a title of honour which he would use of other patriarchates; and that he did not consider the power

of the patriarchates as unalterable is seen by his
attempted creation of the new jurisdiction of his own
city Justiniana Prima (Tauresium), a few miles south
of Sofia, over a large district. To the archbishop whom
he here created he gave authority to "hold the place
of the apostolic throne" within his province.[1]

This position, then, of the Byzantine patriarchate,
as independent of the other patriarchates, and equal
to that of the older Rome, but occupying in
point of honour a secondary position, was
recognised by Church and State alike; and
it was this that the Council *in Trullo* re-
affirmed. In another point it was divergent from Rome—that of the marriage of the clergy.
Subdeacons, deacons, and priests were forbidden to
marry, but those married before ordination were equally
forbidden, under pain of excommunication, to separate
from their wives.

An attempt of the mad emperor Justinian II. to
enforce the acceptance of the decrees by Pope Sergius I.
was a complete failure. Popes were becoming much
stronger in Italy than was the distant Cæsar.
Rome was becoming independent of emperor and of
exarch alike. In 711 the pope Constantine visited
Constantinople as an honoured guest, where he was
treated with diplomatic politeness, and where, possibly
after they had undergone modification, he signed the

Indepen-
dent
attitude of
Constan-
tinople.

[1] See Procopius, *De Ædif.*, iv. 1 (ed. Bonn., pp. 266, 267); and
Novellae, xi. (de privilegiis archiepiscopi primæ Justinianæ) and
cxxxi. (de ecclesiasticis canonibus et privilegiis), cap. 3. It is no
alteration of patriarchal powers, but rather the assertion of them.
Still patriarchal jurisdictions are not regarded as unalterable—as
is clear from the creation of the modern national churches of the
Balkan lands.

decrees of the Trullian Council. On this point the papal biographer is silent, but he asserts with enthusiasm the reverence of the emperor for the pope and the latter's regret when the bloody tyrant met the reward of his crimes a few weeks later. With this the ecclesiastical interest of Eastern history is for a time in the background.

CHAPTER VIII

THE CHURCH IN ASIA

IN the East Christianity had spread to Persia from
Edessa.[1] The Parthians seem to have put no
obstacle in its way, but when the Persians came into
conflict with the Roman Empire, now Christian, there
was long and bitter persecution. At last The
toleration was reached, after Sapor II., and Church in
from the beginning of the fourth century Persia.
the Church in Persia was organised, and governed
by many bishops; the primate took the title of
Catholicos and had his see at Seleucia, and had
suffragans on both sides of the Persian Gulf. In
Assyria and Chaldæa the mass of the population
became Christians, and Christians were spread, less
thickly, over Media, Khorassan, and Persia itself.
The dignity of the Persian catholicos was considerable; he might be compared with the Byzantine
patriarchs, and the Church almost occupied the position of an established religion, related to the civil
power. But the distance, and the constant wars
between the Empire and Persia, tended inevitably to
separate the Churches. From the end of the fifth
century the Church in Persia, surrendered to Nestorian-

[1] See *The Church of the Fathers* (vol. ii. of the present series),
chapter xxix., for the earlier history.

ism, had begun visibly to decay. It was controlled by
the Persian kings, it was a prey to endless controversy
and intrigue, and when the Persian kingdom was at
war with the Empire it was in grave danger. It
held councils furtively; it passed canons, and, itself
heretical, condemned other and more recent heresies
than its own. But often its catholicos engaged in
the dynastic politics of the Persian dynasties, and
Christianity, regarded as one among many religions,
and tainted with the same materialism as the rest,
sank into impotence and was torn by schism. Meanwhile, in the neighbourhood of the Persian realm,
Christianity was spreading.

Many barbarous tribes during Justinian's reign were
admitted to the Christian faith and fellowship. The
Growth of the Church under Justinian. Tzani dwelling on the border of Armenia
and Pontus, "separated from the sea by
precipitous mountains and vast solitudes,
impassable torrent beds and yawning
chasms,"[1]—in a land where, Procopius tells us,[2] "it
is not possible to irrigate the ground, to reap a crop,
or to find a meadow anywhere; and even the trees
bear no fruit, because for the most part there is no
regular succession of seasons, and the land is not at
one time subjected to cold and wet, and at another
made fertile by the warmth of the sun, but is
desolated by perpetual winter and covered by eternal
snows. They changed their religion to the true faith,
became Christians, and embraced a more civilised
mode of life." The king of those Heruls who served
in the Roman army, and a Hunnish king, Gordas,

[1] Bury, *History of the Later Roman Empire*, i. 441.
[2] *Ædif.*, iii. 6.

became Christians. The Abasgi (or Albagrians) of
the Caucasus were converted, and for the most part
remained associated with the Armenians and the
Iberians of Georgia,[1] "when they were compelled by
the Persian king to worship idols," put themselves
under the imperial protection, and they remained
closely in connection with the Armenian Church till
608,[when they accepted the decisions of Chalcedon.
They remained independent and orthodox till their
union, a century ago, with the Russian Church.

In Armenia, similarly, had grown up a national
Church, which had a catholicos, a hierarchy, a
vernacular liturgy of its own. When in   Separation
the middle of the fifth century the ancient   from the
kingdom was split up between the Empire   Church.
and the Persians, the Armenian Church still remained
apart. Its national features were strongly marked
even before dogmatic differences arose. With the
Nestorian and Monophysite heresies new divisions
took place. The Persians gradually, between 435 and
480, accepted Nestorianism, and in 483 definitely
separated from the Catholic Church, and Nisibis became a school of Nestorian theology. The Armenians
survived this danger but were led into Monophysitism,
and in 505 they pronounced against the Council of
Chalcedon. Their theology became tainted with
further heresy in the sixth century, and they are still
separate from the orthodox Church of the East.
Thus, at the time with which we have to deal, as
we have said, Christianity east of Antioch and on
the borders of Persia was under Nestorian influence.
After 431 Nestorianism became gradually established

[1] Joannes Biclarensis p. 853.

as the dominant creed. The Church of the East, as it
was officially called, rejected the Third General Council,
and was cut off from the Catholic Church. It long
remained a strong body. The great schools of Nisibis,
Edessa, and Baghdad were centres of religion, learning, and civilisation.

The Nestorians [1] "also sent out missionaries northward among the wandering Tartar tribes and along the
shores of the Caspian; southward to Persia,
The Nestorians. India, and Ceylon; and eastward across
the steppes of Central Asia into China.
The bilingual inscription of Singanfu, in Chinese and
Syriac, relates that Nestorian missionaries laboured in
China as far back as A.D. 636.[2] In the sixth and
seventh centuries the Church of the East could count
its twenty-five metropolitans or archbishops; and the
number and remoteness of their sees, stretching from
Jerusalem to China, testifies to her missionary zeal.
Those who dwelt nearest to Baghdad met the
catholicos in yearly synod; those farthest off sent
their confession of faith to him every sixth year.

By the Middle Ages the Church of the East had
spread over the whole of Central Asia. The curious
legends of the powerful kingdom of Prester
Prester John and his con- version. John, somewhere in the heart of Asia, grew
out of the conversion, by Nestorian mer-
chants in the eleventh century, of a certain
King of Kerait, a kingdom of Tartary to the north
of China. This king is said to have requested that
missionaries might be sent to him from the Church

---

[1] I quote from the admirable summary in the Reports of the Archbishop's Mission to the Assyrian Christians

[2] See an interesting account in Williams's *Middle Kingdom.*

of his converters; and, when they were come, these missionaries baptized him, naming him John,[1] and he was ordained priest (Presbyter or Prester). Two hundred thousand people of the nation embraced Christianity; the successors to the kingdom bore the dynastic name of John, and were ordained priests. However uhcertain this story is, the fact of the conversion of the princes of Kerait in Tartary is sufficiently well established. The prosperity of the Church of the East culminated in the eleventh century. The khalifs of Baghdad protected their Christian subjects, and important offices of state were often filled by them.

Height of
prosperity.

The Indian Church, which was believed to date back to the time of S. Thomas the Apostle, had probably its origin in Nestorian missions, and accepted Monophysite opinions.

As we have seen, the wider field of missionary work owed much to the labours of the Nestorians. It is possible that Cosmas,[2] who had travelled far afield in the first half of the sixth century, may have been a Nestorian; but the reverence with which he speaks of the orthodox faith, and his constant use of the Catholic writers, would seem to show rather that, when he became a monk at any rate, he was orthodox. From him, however, we obtain knowledge of the wide field of Nestorian missions. Recent discoveries have largely added to our knowledge. It is clear that in the sixth century,

Their
missions.

---

[1] His name was Ung; his title Khan ; Ung Khan was Syriacised into Yukhanan, i.e. John.

[2] The *Christian Topography* was written between 535 and 537. Beazley, *Dawn of Modern Geography*, p. 279.

H

apparently before 540, Nestorian bishoprics were
founded in Herat and Samarkand. Monumental inscriptions date back as far as 547. Merv, as early as

650, is spoken of as a "falling church"[1]

in the Far East. amid the triumphs of Islam. China has
been already mentioned, and though it is
not clear that only Nestorian missions prospered in
the far land, there is no doubt that their success was
the most prominent. Christian communities existed
near the borders of Tibet[2] in the seventh century; and
in the eighth and ninth they were strong in India.
Even in the eleventh century the "Nestorian worship
retained a great hold over many parts of Asia, between
the Euphrates and the Gobi desert." Into the later
and fragmentary history of these missions it is not
here the place to enter. Let it only be remembered
that the labours of "those Nestorian missionaries who
preached and baptized under the shadow of the wall
of China, and on the shores of the Yellow Sea, the
Caspian, and the Indian Ocean"[3] were made possible
by the diplomatic and military triumphs which radi-
ated from Constantinople in the sixth century, and
by the Christian zeal of orthodox emperors and patriarchs.

Meanwhile in Persia the Monophysites contended
for supremacy with the Nestorians, and organised

Nestorian-ism in Persia. themselves with considerable skill. But
the Nestorians, who founded schools and
developed a Christology on lines different
from those on which European thought was proceed-

---

[1] Assemani, *Bibl. Orient*, iii. i. 130, 131.
[2] See Waddell, *Buddhism in Tibet*, pp. 421, 422.
[3] Beazley, *Dawn of Modern Geography*, p. 211.

ing, became still more rigid in their rejection of the Catholic teaching. Maraba the catholicos (540-52) and Thomas of Edessa, his pupil, seem to have drawn very near to orthodoxy; but the controversy of the Three Chapters widened the breach. Council after council, theologian, catholicos, monastery, bishop, alike denounced Justinian; and they had the support of the pagan philosophers whom he had expelled from the schools of Athens.

In Persia monasticism and the life of hermits— though the introduction of either is difficult if not impossible to trace [1]—flourished and developed on lines of their own. For a long time there was no distinction between monastic and secular life : it was only gradually that an organised monasticism grew up out of the cœnobitic life for men and for women. But from the sixth century onward the organisation of monasticism gave strength to the Church, and enabled it for some time to resist the Muhammadan invasion. The Church, mapped out into dioceses and well served by numerous clergy, and having its own canon law, its own liturgical forms, and its own theology, was able for long, in spite of the absence of all state support and in spite often of state persecution, to survive in some appearance of strength till the Muhammadan invasion. The Mussulman conquest, when once it was achieved, gave something like security to the Nestorians. Though there was a time of persecution in the ninth century, it was short. Christians as teachers, physicians, philosophers, were famous in the foundation of the learning of the palmy days of the khalifs. But the whole

[1] Cf. Budge, *The Book of Governors*, i. cxvi., and Labourt, *Le Christianisme dans l'empire perse*, 303.

structure fell before the invasions, in later days, of the Mongols and the Turks.

From the more distant parts of the Persian Empire **The Church in Palestine.** we may pass to the land where the Church had its birth. During the period of revived power in the Empire, Palestine was at peace under Justinian's rule.

In Jerusalem itself [1] it is chiefly to be said that the emperor engaged in large restorations and some original church building after the style of his better known work. He had a severe struggle with the Samaritans, but it led to many conversions.[2]

But here, as elsewhere, as time went on the encroachments of the Persians were a perpetual danger to the **Conquest by the Persians.** Christianity of the East. In 615 Jerusalem fell into their hands. The Jews, whom earlier emperors had, like Justinian, kept in subjection, had grown in the days of Heraclius to be much more powerful in Syria than the Christians, and it was they who secured Jerusalem and gave it into the hands of the Persians; and again, after the Christians had overpowered the garrison, the city was given back to them and to scenes of pillage and outrage; the churches, so splendid as early as the fourth century, and described in glowing language by Procopius in the sixth, were sacked and defiled; the clergy and the patriarch were made captive; the Holy Cross, discovered by the Empress Helena, was sent away into Persia; and "all these things," says the chronicler, "happened not in a year or a month, but within a few days." The ruined churches were, however, restored

---

[1] Cf. Procopius, *Ædif.;* and John Moschus, *Pratum Spirituale* (Migne, *Patr. Græc.*, lxxxvii. [3]). [2] Procopius, *Ædif.*, v. 8.

THE CHURCH IN ASIA

101

before long by the alms of the faithful, and it was not long before the Christians themselves were favoured by the Persian king, and Chosroes, in consequence of a council at Jerusalem in 628, legalised, it would seem, the Monophysite heresy as the representative of Christianity. The conquest of Egypt followed on that of Syria; and the union of the Coptic Church with that of the Syrian Monophysites was a result, natural and almost inevitable, of the community of suffering between them. Within a few years—his campaign began in 622—the heroic emperor Heraclius won back all that had been lost, utterly defeated the Persians, won back the Holy Rood, restored the patriarch Zacharias to Jerusalem, and returned in triumph to the imperial city. In 629 he went on a pilgrimage to the Holy City, and on September 14th—still observed as the feast of the Exaltation of the Holy Cross—he restored the Rood to the Church of the Resurrection.

Recon- quest by Heraclius, 622.

In the year 610 Muhammad began his career as a prophet. It is no part of Church history to trace the origin of his opinions or his power, to tell how he learnt from Jews and Nestorians, or how he established a marvellous organisation on a basis of theocratic militarism. The migration from Meccah to Medinah in 622 was the beginning of his active ministry, of religious teaching carried forward by sword and fire. The capture of Meccah, the submission of Arabia, the extinction of the Christian (Monophysite) communities in the peninsula, were followed before long by the invasion of Syria and the capture of Jerusalem by the Khalif Omar in 637. The year before, Heraclius

Conquest by the Muham- madans.

had taken away the Holy Rood and the treasures of the churches to Constantinople. Two years later the Muhammadans seized Egypt, from which the Persians had not so long been driven out by the armies of the Empire. The fatal policy of the Monothelite emperors had opened the way to the triumph of Islam. Of this we shall see more, in Africa and in Southern Europe, in later days.

CHAPTER IX

THE CHURCH IN AFRICA

IN the middle of the fifth century the Christian power in North Africa fell under the domination of the Arian Vandals. S. Augustine died in 430 while the foe was at the gates of his city. In 439 Carthage fell, and Roman civilisation was extinguished. The rule of the Vandals was not only Arian but barbarous. It is not unlikely that their victory was won with the aid of the remaining Donatists and the heathen Moors. With the reign of Gaiseric some degree of toleration was allowed to the Catholic Church, but the persecution which had marked the earlier days of the Arian power now took the form of confiscation and the suppression of public worship. The Church suffered grievously, and not least in the class of persons ordained to the ministry and consecrated to the episcopate. But still the Catholics were the great majority, and it was seen that the Arian Vandals were in danger of absorption by the subtle influence of the truth. It was a last effort of Gaiseric's to deprive the Catholics of their leaders, which eventually brought about their restoration. The Bishop of Carthage and several of his clergy were put on board a ship and told to escape whither they could. They reached Naples, and their piteous plight and the news they brought

The Vandal persecution. helped to direct the attention of the imperial power to its lost heritage. Meanwhile the suffering Church, enjoying now a scanty toleration, now suffering a severer persecution, continued to make converts and to produce martyrs. In 477 Gaiseric died. A year before his death he had allowed the Catholics to reopen their churches and to bring back their bishops and clergy from exile. And still their missionary efforts had never been relaxed. Church life still continued; inscriptions remaining to-day preserve the epitaphs of men buried in the darkest days with Catholic rites; and in the interior ancient monasteries remained undisturbed. Hunneric, the next Vandal king, though nominally an Arian, set himself to extirpate heresies which he did not accept: Manichæans under his sway received treatment more severe than Catholics. Indeed, the Catholics began to raise their heads under the leadership of Eugenius, who was elected in 479 to the see of Carthage, the only bishopric in the country which held metropolitan rank. The Bishop of Carthage was the spiritual head of the whole province, held a superiority over the bishops outside the limits of Proconsularis, and was, as it were, the patriarch of the African Church. For twenty-three years the see had had no pastor, and the restoration marked a distinct step towards the ending of the Vandal domination. But there was a final effort; Hunneric, unable to decoy the Catholics, determined to exterminate them; a writer of the time tells that nearly five thousand clergy were banished to the desert, where their fate was a practical martyrdom. A conference was sum-

moned in 484, at which it was endeavoured to make
the Catholic clergy abate the strictness of their
orthodoxy, but Eugenius stood firm. Persecution again
followed. The writer already mentioned, Victor
Vitensis, says, " The Vandals did not blush to set forth
against us the law which formerly our Christian
emperors had passed against them and other heretics
for the honour of the Catholic Church, adding many
things of their own as it pleased their tyrannical
power." Thus evil deeds bring their necessary consequences. A bitter persecution swept over the land,
and till the death of Hunneric, at the end of the year,
atrocities of the most terrible kind were perpetrated.
It was a brief age of martyrs, and rooted the Church
more firmly in the affections of its children. It was
an age, too, of saints, and Fulgentius shines out by the
side of Eugenius as a pattern of Christian devotion
and asceticism. In the years that followed king succeeded king, and the condition of the Church became
gradually more tolerable, till under Hilderic much of
the old organisation was restored and the monastic
houses were established in a condition of considerable
independence. When Gelimer usurped the Vandal
throne, the power of Justinian was able to intervene,
and in 533 Belisarius recovered North
Africa for the Empire. The restoration of
the direct rule of the emperors was of
necessity the restoration of Catholicism to
dominance. But materially the Church had received
blows from which she never fully recovered. Her
possessions, buildings, treasures had for the most part
passed from her hands : and many sees, many parishes,

Reconquest
of Africa by
Belisarius,
533.

still remained without pastors. Such was the result of " the violent captivity of a century."

Justinian aimed at restoring all things to their first estate. "We would be the guardians and defenders of the ancient traditions," he wrote in 542 to the primate of Byzacene. He confirmed the Bishop of Carthage in his metropolitan dignity; he restored sees, allowed synods to meet, gave special privileges to the clergy. An era of church building set in, and fine

The revival of the North African Church. monasteries were erected, in all the impressive solidity of the Byzantine style, even in distant parts of the Roman territory. Tebessa remains a marvellous example of the wealth and dignity which came anew to the North African Church. The literary power of the Church revived with her material prosperity: a school of writers arose again in the land of Augustine. Primasius, Facundus, Liberatus, Victor of Tonnenna, were among those who restored the activity and knowledge of the Church in history, theology, and apologetic. Over all the emperor Justinian kept his watchful eye, directing, interfering, exhorting, as seemed to him good. The controversy of the Three Chapters had its echoes in Africa, and the deacon Ferrand, a learned theologian, represented a very wide feeling when, in his *Defensio*, he deprecated any condemnation of the dead theologians; and in Facundus, Bishop of Hermiane, the unhappy hesitating pope Vigilius found an adviser who, if anyone, might have given him firmness. In the result, the emperor, by the pen at least as much as the sword, overpowered resistance, and Africa accepted the decisions of Constantinople. Reparatus, Bishop of Carthage, who resisted, was deposed, Liber-

atus preserves the record of bitter persecution, and
Victor of Tonnenna, who equally refused to accept the
decision against the Three Chapters, is especially bitter
in his denunciation of Justinian. But the pope Pelagius was able, in 560, to announce the assent of Africa
to the statements of the Fifth General Council. The
Church from the death of Justinian settled down in
peaceable habitations, strong in the imperial support
and the affection of the people. But as, in the relaxation which set in as time went on, the power of the
imperial administration decayed, the power of the
popes in Africa was gradually strengthened, and
the power of the bishops rose equally. But this was
not all. In time relaxation set in in the Church as well
as in the State. There are tales of immoral and corrupt
bishops, of disobedience to authority, of a recrudes-
cence, from 591 to 596, of Donatism. It was the pope
Gregory the Great who took in hand the needed
reformation. His letters are full of African affairs:
his keen attention, his instructions to Hilarus, the
administrator of the Roman Church's possessions in
Italy, his minute knowledge, his wise understanding of the many difficult problems
which beset the Church, are prominent
in his correspondence. It was he who re-
versed the conception of Justinian in regard to the
Church of North Africa. The emperor had striven for
orthodoxy, without the supremacy of the pope. Gregory
was determined to secure the latter, and the history
of North Africa affords an excellent example of how
the papal power grew. It was by continual intervention, in affairs small as well as great, and by
constant solicitude: it was by the use of prudent

Its
relation to
Gregory
the Great.

and sympathetic agents, and the firm adherence to a policy of charity, orthodoxy and discretion, that the great pope enforced his views on the bishops, the Church, the imperial representatives. While he sternly rebuked all abuse of the political authority which had fallen into the hands of the bishops, he tenaciously clung to the right of hearing appeals in cases between churchmen and public officials which circumstances had placed in his hands. From a right of control he passed to a right of direct intervention; and in State as well as Church the administrators felt the power of his indomitable will. While disorganisation was spreading in the civil order the Church was growing in concentration and authority.

But the Monothelite controversy went far to shatter the power which the labour of Gregory had built up, and with it the Christianity of Northern Africa. The orthodox felt less and less bound to emperors who supported heresy, and the Arab invasion drew near without the people perceiving the full extent of their danger. Fortunatus, Bishop of Carthage, declared himself a Monothelite, but in every other province besides his the Church formally repudiated the heresy. In 646 Fortunatus was deposed and Victor succeeded him; and this is almost the last recorded incident in the history of the North African Church. As the Arab invader advanced, refugees from Syria and Egypt poured into the land, and, since many of them were heretical, added to the religious diffusions of the country. The abbat Maximus upheld the banner of orthodoxy against all comers. The victory which he won over the heresiarch Pyrrhus in 645, followed by the declarations of

The Monothelite controversy.

provincial synods in 646, was the last expression of African orthodoxy.

John, the Jacobite bishop of Nikiu, whose contemporary account of the Saracen conquest is of the first value, declares that "everyone said that the expulsion of the Romans and the victory of the Mussulmans were brought about by the tyranny of the emperor Heraclius and the troubles which he made the orthodox suffer." A general discontent with the Byzantine government arose, and Rome, which was more in sympathy with the people, was unable to help them. In 646 the patrician Gregory, the imperial governor, orthodox and a protector of the Church, declared that the Monothelite Constans II. had forfeited the throne, and assumed for himself the title of emperor. Within a year he was defeated and slain by the Saracens at Sbeitla, and Byzantine Africa was placed at the mercy of the Muhammadan invader. The Copts long resisted, but their resistance was overcome in the autumn of 646. Alexandria fell a second time and finally into the hands of the Arabs.

For fifty years the Byzantine power maintained a foothold, precarious and nominal. Inch by inch, and with intervals of repose and even of reconquest,—as when John the Patrician, under Leo the Isaurian, recaptured Carthage,— the infidels advanced, and the Berber tribes of the interior pressed, too, upon the Christians. Carthage was again taken by the Muhammadans in 698 : the native tribes joined the invaders, and by 708 Roman Africa was wholly in their hands. Toleration was at first allowed; but from 717 the Christians had only the choice of banishment and

The conquest by the Muhammadans.

apostasy. Still many held out: Christian villages remained, Christian communities, as late as the fourteenth century; and even now it is said that in some parts Christian customs survive. The Church at Carthage existed certainly in some organised form till the eleventh century, and it was not till 1583 that the Church of Tunis was utterly destroyed.

Meanwhile events in other parts of Africa had run a different course. The patriarchate of Alexandria had a long and distinguished history, and from it had spread missions far into the south.

The Monophysite controversy led to the founding of the Jacobite sect. Secret consecrations at Constantinople by bishops in prison during Justinian's severe rule sent a bishop to Hira for the Arabian Christians in Persia, and another to the borders of Edessa, who founded the Jacobites and with the assistance of Egyptian Monophysite bishops continued the episcopal succession. In Egypt there arose the division between the Melkites, who followed the imperial orders and accepted the decisions of the Councils, and the Copts, who dissented. The Monophysites of Syria, Egypt, and Armenia, with temporary and superficial differences, remained practically at one. National differences confirmed their divergence from the Roman Empire and the Catholic Church. Thus while in Egypt, Syria, and elsewhere the Church was still powerfully represented, though side by side with strong sectarian organisations, there were, when the followers of Muhammad came to add to the confusion, three nationalistic and heretical bodies, separate from the Church—those of Persia and Armenia and Ethiopia. Of the last something must now be said.

The Jacobites.

South of Egyptian territory, properly so called, lay
the Ethiopians, vassals of Egypt, tracing in a dim
fashion their Christianity back to one of   The
those queens who bore the title of *Candace.* Abyssinian
These wild and warring tribes kept up con- Church.
tinual conflict, and among the Blemmyes men still
worshipped Isis in the temple of Philae. In 548 began
the conversion of the Nobadae of the Soudan, of whose
reception into the Christian fold the great Monophysite
missionary, John of Ephesus, gives an account. Churches
were built, and one inscription at least survives with
the name of a Christian king. Beyond them the
Alodaei learnt the faith from the same preacher,
Longinus. Nubia, or Mugurrah, was also visited by
Christian missionaries at the same time. Under
Justinian, the temple of Philae was turned into a church,
and the Blemmyes became Christian. Christian remains long existed, even down to the neighbourhood of
Khartoum ; and it was long before the Muhammadan
conquerors swept all the worship of Christ away.
Further south Christianity spread on both sides of the
Red Sea. In Arabia Felix was the kingdom of the
Homerites or Himyarites, whose chief city was Safar,
and at different times they were ruled by the same king
as the land of Axum, " the farthest Ind" of the Greek
chronicler Theophanes. After the dispersion, Jewish
colonies settled in Arabia, and in the fourth century
Christianity followed. At the end of the fifth century
a bishop is found among the Homerites, and a Trini-
tarian inscription is dated 542–3. About the same
time the Church in Abyssinia, founded in the time of
S. Athanasius, received the national religion of the
country through the conversion of the Negus at the end

of the fifth century. While the land of Safar at times relapsed into heathenism and massacred Christians, the Abyssinians remained firm in the faith. Procopius tells that Ellesthaeos, an Ethiopian king, during the reign of Justin I., invaded the land of the Homerites to avenge their persecutions and to suppress the Jewish predominance and set up a Christian king. With him and his successors Justinian entered into treaties, as also with the kings of Axum or Abyssinia. While the Muhammadan conquest swept away the Christianity of the Arabians and drove those who clung to it northward to the banks of the Euphrates, the Church in Abyssinia, which had accepted Monophysitism, remained independent, just as its mother church of Egypt obtained toleration. It still continues separate, Monophysite, and in communion with the Coptic Church of Egypt.

CHAPTER X

THE CHURCH IN THE WESTERN ISLES

WHEN Gregory the Great sent Augustine and
his brother monks to preach to the Teutonic
tribes which had made Britain their home, there were
already two Churches in the island. There was the
Church of the Brythons, gradually separated Christian-
by the advance of the Saxons into the ity in
Churches of Cumbria or Strathclyde, Wales, Britain.
and West Wales or Cornwall. These stood apart from
the English for a long time, were late in accepting the
Catholic customs of the West, and had no influence on
the progress of English Christianity. And there was
the Church founded in North Britain by Celtic missionaries from Ireland. In Ireland there seems little
doubt that Christianity was known by the end of the
fourth century. In the fifth century the progress
was extraordinarily rapid. S. Patrick "organised the
Christianity which already existed; he converted kingdoms which were still pagan, especially in the west;
and he brought Ireland into connection with the
Church of the Empire, and made it formally part of
Universal Christendom."[1]

The subsequent history of the Church in Ireland
forms a fit introduction to that of the Church in

[1] Bury, *Life of S. Patrick*, pp. 212-13.

England, in spite of the separation between them. Irish Christianity did not long preserve its close union with Western Europe. The popes, as well as the emperors, were too weak to interfere in the distant islands. The Irish relapsed into the use of what is called the Celtic Easter, and to other practices which were usual before Patrick's day and which served to cut them off from the newly-converted **Death of** Teutons, as well as from the Latin world **S. Patrick,** in general. Patrick died in 461. In 563 **461.** Columba, trained in the great schools which had sprung up in the Irish monasteries, crossed to what is now called Scotland to confirm the faith of the Irish settlers and to convert the heathen Picts. The organisation of the Church to which he belonged was **The** essentially tribal and monastic. Though **Celtic** S. Patrick had probably consecrated dio- **Church.** cesan bishops in large numbers, the Church soon became "predominantly monastic." Tribal feeling was so strong that the Church, too, assimilated itself to the tribal idea, and the Church's monasteries were her tribes. In a land where there were no cities monasteries took their place, and the bishops naturally came to dwell in them, and so to seem less prominent in their episcopal than in their monastic aspect. The monks became the chief power in Christian Ireland; and in the sixth, seventh, and eighth centuries there were many bishops without dioceses, and it seems probable that their rank, though not their function, was less important than that of the abbats, the heads of the tribal monasticism.

In the seventh century again the Irish Church came back into closer association with the Church throughout

Europe. This union was due very largely to the influence of learning, and still more to the influence of missionary zeal. "From Iceland to the Danube or the Apennines, among Frank or Burgundian or Lombard, the Irish energy seemed omnipotent and inexhaustible."[1] Into Ireland it would seem that classical culture was introduced by the first Christian teachers, and that from the first it was intended to serve as a preparation for religious teaching.[2] It would seem that it was from Brittany that it spread to Ireland. The schools of Ireland became famous. Books as diverse as the Antiphonary of Bangor and Adamnan's Life of Columba show that the teaching in its different ways was a sound and a liberal one.

The influences outside Ireland

In England the Irish tradition and influence spread. If the Celtic school of Bangor perished in the stress of the bitter wars between English and Welsh, Mal- mesbury, which trained S. Aldhelm, showed that the Irish love of letters was capable of transplantation into a land now most prominently Teutonic. But the Roman influence and the influence of the East were still more effective. Benedict Biscop brought back with him to Northum- bria the traditions and rules of Italian art and learning, and Theodore of Tarsus brought a wider influence, which was Greek as well as Latin. He himself founded a school at Canterbury, and taught it; and in distant times Dunstan, at Glastonbury and at Canterbury, was his worthy successor. In the north Bede was at

in learning,

[1] R. L. Poole, Illustrations of the History of Medieval Thought, p. 10.

[2] Cf. Roger, L'Enseignement des lettres classiques, p. 236.

Jarrow a writer of great power and wide scope, and the school of York was a nursery of classic studies which produced the great scholar Alcuin. Thus the community of scholarship brings the Churches together.

More prominent was the zeal for the conversion of the heathen. The work of Columban and of S. Gall had its origin in the Irish schools, and there was no more fruitful influence on the Europe of the Dark

in mission-
ary work. Age. The work of Columba and his followers was to begin in the north of Britain what Roman missionaries undertook in the south. For more than thirty years Columba, who landed in Iona in 563, taught the Picts and Scots. His Life by his disciple Adamnan is one of the most beautiful memorials of medieval saintliness that we possess. The monastery which he founded lasted till the eighth century. His school did a famous work in North Britain in the seventh; King Oswald of Northumbria was trained there, and S. Aidan, his fellow-helper, the typical saint of Northumbria. From the same source came Melrose, the great Scottish monastery, and S. Chad, the apostle of the Middle English.

A century of intermittent strife swept over the north-

Scotland. ern lands. Scotland became Christian slowly and with little connection with the south. Heathen onslaughts ravaged the Christian lands, and yet, in spite of all, monasteries for men and women sprang up in the north. The influence of S. Aidan (died 651) was continued by S. Cuthbert and S. Hilda, typical parents of monks and nuns. In 664 (Synod of Whitby) at last came union with the Church of the English, who appealed to the authority of Rome and

of S. Peter in favour of their customs, and the
Northumbrian king, Oswiu, ratified the union of the
Celtic and the English Churches. Early in the eighth
century other Celtic Churches came into the agreement; only Cornwall held out for two centuries more.

The English Church, which thus came to represent
the Christianity of the whole island, was founded from
Rome by S. Augustine in Kent in 597. It   The mis-
was from the first an active missionary   sion of S.
body. It gradually won its way over the   Augustine,
whole island, conquering and assimilating   597.
the alien influences which were at first opposed to it.
So when a storm of heathen persecution swept over
England and Scotland at the end of the eighth
century, when " the ravaging of heathen men lament-
ably destroyed God's church at Lindisfarne," when
the monks of Iona were given to martyrdom, when
English prelates and kings gave their lives to hold
the land for Christ, the Church still endured, with
material loss but with, for the time at least, enhanced
glory and virtue. Three names stand out conspicuously
from the seventh and ninth centuries. Theodore of
Tarsus, Archbishop of Canterbury from 668 to 693,
was the great organiser of the English   Theodore
Church. A scholar, a teacher, a statesman,   of Tarsus,
he knit the different tribes of English,   668.
Saxon, Jute, together in the unity of faith and discipline. Church councils sprang up under him to rule,
and Church laws to guide men in the way. He kept
up a close connection with the Western Church, but
he did not surrender independence to a papal supremacy. Wilfrith of Ripon, his contemporary, was great
also as a teacher and as a missionary beyond the seas,

and among the Saxons of South Britain. The seventh century was the age in which the foundations of the English Church were laid on firm bases.

Hardly less important, though in a different way, was the work of the monk Baeda, the father of English history. He was a man who knew the history and the theology of the Western Church, and who taught by his writings and his life. His influence on the development of the Church in the north, both by his great history, his religious treatises, and his influence on Egbert, Archbishop of York, is incalculable.

Bede.

The age of Alfred, who died in 899, was equally important. It witnessed a more distinct union with the Church of Wales, whose glories go back to the time of S. David in the fifth century. It confirmed a strong union between Church and State in England, and it witnessed a revival of Christian learning in which Alfred himself and a Welshman, Asser, whom he made bishop of an English see, were the leaders. Alfred was a bright example of what Christianity could do for mankind. Warrior, scholar, saint, pattern king whose heart was given to his people, he bore himself nobly before the world as one who loved and worshipped the Master Christ. Under his sway the Church rose again to instruct and guide the people, and when he died he left the English land a united Christian nation. The Danes, who after years of predatory invasion were become settlers over a large part of England, were brought into the Church; and the British Church in Cornwall was brought nearer to unity with the English, a union which was complete from 931.

Alfred.

While in the extreme north, Ross, Cromarty, Sutherland, and Caithness, the Church remained missionary rather than parochial, in the Scotland of the south monasticism became prominent again under a new order called, in Goidelic, "Culdees" (servants of God). In the midlands years of disturbance caused much of the organisation of the Church to disappear, bishoprics to cease, monasteries to be destroyed. After the Danish wars the work of reconstruction was an urgent need, and a great prelate came to lead it.

Conversion of the north.

Dunstan (924-88) was a West Saxon who was taught at Glastonbury by Irish priests, and who rose, through his friendship with leaders in Church and State, by the holiness of his life, and by the experience that he won when in exile in Flanders, to be head of the English Church. As archbishop he was "a true shepherd." He gave up all the preferments he had before enjoyed, only visiting Glastonbury occasionally for a time of repose. His friends, Æthelwold, Bishop of Winchester, and Oswald, Bishop of Worcester, with King Eadgar's help, did their utmost to introduce the strict rule of S. Benedict into the monasteries, replacing the clergy of the cathedral churches (secular canons) by monks. Dunstan sympathised, but he did not actively support their action. Abroad there was strong feeling against clerical marriage, and there were many canons passed against it. The danger of the Church falling into the hands of an hereditary class of officials was a real one; but it does not seem to have been much felt in England. Dunstan paid far more heed to the clergy's books than their wives.

Dunstan, 924-88.

He made rules, and encouraged schools for the training of priests. He ordered priests to learn handicrafts

His work that they might teach them to others. He
as arch- ordered that a sermon should be preached in
bishop and each church every Sunday. His zeal for
reformer. moral reform was seen in many canons
passed against the abuses of the age, and he did not
hesitate to enforce them against the highest in the
land. When the pope ordered him to absolve a great
lord whom he had excommunicated for an unlawful
marriage, he refused to obey.

Early in the tenth century an illustration of the
position occupied by the English Church in relation to
Rome, and of the learning of its clergy and their style
of preaching, is afforded by the writings of Ælfric, who
described himself in his early years as " a monk and a
mass-priest," and was later on abbat of Eynsham. Of
his work, besides educational treatises, eighty sermons,
chiefly translated from the Latin, remain. In them he
shows clearly that the claims of the papacy with regard to S. Peter were not accepted by all in England,
and he taught the spiritual, not corporal, presence of
the Lord's Body in the Holy Communion. The English
Church differed also from Rome in the fact that many
of the clergy were married, and though this was not
regarded as lawful, they were not separated from their
wives. But in all essential matters the English
Church remained in union with the foreign Churches
and retained her ancient reputation for unbroken
orthodoxy. This reputation was increased by the fame
of S. Dunstan, whose sojourn abroad had served to
link English churchmen again to their brothers over
sea.

The last years of the great archbishop were given to prayer and study, and to the arts of music and handicraft which he had practised in his youth. He set himself to train the young, to succour the needy, and to make peace among all men. He died on May 19th, 988, and with him the new energy he had infused into the Church seemed to pass away. New Danish invasions turned men's thoughts other ways, but still monasteries made progress. The Benedictine rule was accepted over Southern England, and in the north the see of Durham rose replacing the older northern see, when it became the resting-place of the bones of the great missionary, S. Cuthbert. The Danish invasions were not so barbarous now as in earlier days. Some of the Danes were Christians, and it was at Andover that Olaf Trigvason, King of Norway, was confirmed by Bishop Ælfeah, calling King Æthelred father. He went back to Norway a Christian devoted to the conversion of his people.¹

The English Church at the beginning of the eleventh century was in full communion with the Western Church, but was practically to a large extent apart from papal influence. Church and State walked hand in hand, and the relations between sovereign and archbishop resembled those of the New rather than the Old Rome. The missionary energy which had in former years sent forth Wilfrith and Winfrith was now for the time exhausted. England needed a new religious revival. It came later, at the time of a political conquest.

Meanwhile the Irish Church was regaining its learning and its missionary zeal: both were expressed in

¹ See ch. xi.

the *consuetudo peregrinandi* with which the Irish monks were credited in the ninth century. But from the time of the Danish invasions the Irish Church, and the Welsh also, suffered severely. Heathen settlements in Ireland were only gradually converted, as that of Dublin in 943. The disturbed state of their home encouraged Irish monks to cross the seas. Action and reaction led Ireland more close than ever to the Roman papacy.

CHAPTER XI

THE CONVERSION OF SLAVS AND NORTHMEN

THE ninth century was a great age of conversion, and the work is very largely associated with two great names in the development of civilisation and learning, those of two brothers, born in Thessalonica, probably between 820 and 830—Constan- Cyril and tine (who changed his name to Cyril when Methodius, he was consecrated bishop by Hadrian II. 868. in 868) and Methodius. Their lives show the connection still existing between Rome and the East in Church matters, and illustrate the zeal for educational work which was so conspicuous a feature in the converting energy of the Church of Constantinople. Cyril was not only a priest and a missionary, he was a "philosopher." Methodius, it is said, had been a civil administrator. Both were scholars and linguists, and the influence which they exercised upon the Slavs is incalculably great. In missions always it is the personal influence which is the most striking. But the time is needed as well as the man. So much we see again and again, however cursorily we study the evangelising work of this age.

In missions the ninth century carried out what the eighth neglected or was unable to accomplish. The wars against the Finnish Bulgarians from 755 onwards

The conversion of the Bulgarians.

brought the Church as well as the State into grave danger, or rather were defensive of each. In the eighth century there were several isolated conversions, including a whole family of *boïars* from whom sprang the recluse, saint Joannicius; but there was no general movement. The Bulgarians remained enemies of Christianity and destroyers of all Roman civilisation: S. Theodore of the Studium declared that it was criminal sacrilege to exchange hostages with them. But gradually the geographical nearness brought closer connection: barbarians enlisted in the Roman armies; at last illustrious prisoners in Constantinople were the cause of light being brought to their own land. Boris, the Bulgarian king, obtained teachers from the New Rome, and applied also to Pope Nicolas I. (858–67) for instruction. In 864 the Bulgarians accepted the faith, and the contest for patriarchal rights over them was hotly pressed between Nicolas and Photius, Patriarch of Constantinople (857–86). In the end, after receiving answers from the pope to 106 questions, and after being treated with too little consideration by Hadrian II. (867–72), Boris decided to accept an archbishop from Constantinople in 870, and ten bishoprics were founded.

But the great work of Cyril and Methodius was not directly concerned with the Bulgarian conversion. In

The conversion of the Slavs.

Pannonia and Moravia and Croatia they were the great missionaries to the Slavs. Cyril invented a Slavonic alphabet, and was able to preach to the Slavs everywhere in their own tongue; and in Serbia a flourishing Church sprang up which retained the Slavonic rite. Early in the tenth century many Slavonian priests were ordained by the Bishop of Nona, himself a Slav by birth. But these districts were weakened by incessant strife, and their contests with the East were often fomented by the popes. Their Christianity was distinctly Byzantine; but they were never able to be a real strength to the emperor or the Orthodox Church.

Poland, on the other hand, and later, received its Christianity from a Latin source. There may have been earlier Greek influences through the Slavonic Christians to the south-east; but it was not till 965 that the king, Mieczyslaw, was converted, when he married a Bohemian princess. He became a member of the Empire and the vassal of Otto I. The bishopric of Posen was founded in 968, and the gospel was preached by S. Adalbert, already Bishop of Prague. S. Adalbert, who for a short time held the see of Gnesen, passed on to preach to the heathen Prussians, by whom he was martyred in 997. Otto III. visited the Christian king in A.D. 1000, and gave him a relic, the lance of S. Maurice, still preserved at Cracow. The ecclesiastical organisation of the country was then consolidated; Gnesen was made the metropolitan see, and Polish and Pomeranian dioceses were placed under it. The Latin Church was dominant over Polish Christianity.

Poland.

But the pagan Prussians regarded S. Adalbert as a political emissary and a sorcerer who destroyed their crops, and killed him without hesitation; Bruno, whom Silvester II. sent to succeed him, perished within a year, and the attempt to Christianise the Prussians was

The Prussians and S. Adalbert.

abandoned for nearly two centuries. Similar was
the course of events among the Wends. It is not
till the tenth century that we know anything of
endeavours for their conversion, and then they were
due to the all-embracing energy of Otto I. Henry
I. had borne the royal arms in victory over the
lands watered by the Elbe, the Oder, and the Saale;
and now his successor began the establishment of an
ecclesiastical hierarchy, under the see of Magdeburg.
Boso, Bishop of Merseburg, set himself to learn and
preach in the Slav tongue, but it seems that the
German clergy who were introduced were unsuccessful as missionaries, and won the reputation of greedy
political agitators. At the end of the tenth century
a torrent of pagan fury swept over the land, destroyed
the churches, and stamped the growing Christianity
under foot.

The beginnings of Russian Christianity may possibly
be found, as the patriarch Photius asserted, before the
The con- results of the defeat of the barbarians by
version of John Zimisces. But it was not till nearly
Russia. a century later that anything notable oc-
curred. Olga, a "ruler of Russia," visited Constantinople in 957 and was baptized. Yet the Greek missionaries made but slow progress. It was not till Vladimir
married the sister of the emperor Basil in 989, and
restored the city of Cherson,—in which Cyril more
than a century before had been a missionary,—where he
was baptized, to the Empire, that the evangelisation
of Russia really began. Vladimir deliberately chose
the Greek in preference to the Roman form of Christianity, and acted, it would seem, with some semblance
of national consent. The baptism of the people of

Kiev in the waters of the Dnyepr, as one flock, "some standing in the water up to their necks, others up to their breasts, holding their young children in their arms," was typical of the national acceptance of Christ. Everywhere churches and schools were built and the Slavonic Scriptures taught the people ; at Kiev was built the Church of S. Sophia by Greek masons, in commemoration of the debt to the great Church of the New Rome. Vladimir became the apostle of his people.

S. Vladi-
mir, 989.

The Church pressed forward eagerly, forward over the vast expanse covered by the Russian power, and, not without martyrdoms and tales of heroic adventure, won its way triumphantly to Russian hearts.

The early days of Christianity in Moravia and Bohemia are wrapped in obscurity. In 801 Charles the Great endeavoured a forcible con- version of the former country, but with no more than transitory success. Yet in 836 a church was consecrated at Neutra by the Archbishop of Salzburg. A little later than this we hear of the beginnings of Christian faith among the Czechs. Early Bohemian history, when it emerges from an obscurity lighted by legend, is full of romantic incident. There are passages again and again in its records which for weirdness and ferocity remind us of a grim story of Meinhold's. Paganism lingered there with some of its ancient power, when it had perished, at least outwardly, in all neighbouring lands. In the eleventh century Bohemian heathens still went on pilgrimages to the temple at Arcona on the isle of Rügen, till the practice was stopped by Bretislav II. Still a beginning had been made. In

The
conversion
of the
Czechs.

845 fourteen Bohemian nobles, who had taken refuge at the court of Louis the German, were baptized at Regensburg; but the conversion of the country was to come from the East. Cyril and Methodius, sent by the emperor Michael III. from Constantinople, converted the Moravians, and from them the gospel was handed on to the Czechs. It was Methodius, on whom the pope had conferred the title of Archbishop of Moravia, who baptized the Bohemian prince Bořivoj. For the history of Bohemian Christianity the earliest authority is Kristián, brother of Duke Boleslav II., in *The Life of S. Ludmilla and the Martyrdom of S. Wenceslas.* This is an extremely valuable book, not only as a biography — hagiological, like so much valuable early material for history, yet truthful—and as a record of manners in the tenth century, but as containing the account of the conversion of Moravia to Christianity, which shows that the conversion came first from the East, and the Church long retained a special connection with the Eastern peoples, Bulgarians and Greeks. The account of the murder of S. Wenceslas is of great interest as showing how close was the connection of religion with family and dynastic feuds. S. Ludmilla was murdered in 927 by the orders of her daughter-in-law, who remained a pagan; a year later,[1] her saintly grandson Wenceslas was slain by the men of his evil brother Boleslav. "Holy Wenceslas, who was soon to be a victim for the sake of Christ, rose early, wishing, according to his holy habit, to hurry to the church, that he might remain there for some time in solitary prayer before the congregation arrived;

Saint Wenceslas.

---

[1] According to the chronicle of Kristián.

CONVERSION OF SLAVS AND NORTHMEN 129

and wishing as a good shepherd to hear matins together with his flock, and join in their song, he soon fell into the snares that had been laid," and it was outside the church that he was slain.

It was not till the invasion of the country by the armies of Otto I. in 938 that Christianity was restored even to full toleration, and only when Otto came himself in 950 that it was secured. Boleslav II., the nephew of S. Wenceslas, was named the Pious; and Prague, in 973, was separated from Regensburg and became a bishopric. While among the Moravians the Slavonic rite introduced by Methodius was still largely used, in Bohemia the Roman rite was followed. Voytech (Adalbert), a Czech, was the second bishop, and to him, in spite of failures and difficulties, the conversion of Bohemia was largely due. He died a martyr (as we have said), while preaching to the heathen Prussians, and for a time darkness again settled over the history of the Czechs.

Restor-
ation of
Christian-
ity in
Bohemia.

Meanwhile the current of conversion had spread northwards. It was in 822 that Ebbo, Archbishop of Rheims, was sent to Denmark in consequence of a political embassy to Louis the Pious, emperor from 814 to 840. Harold, the Danish king, had asked aid. The emperor gave him also a Christian teacher; and in 826 the king and his wife were baptized. Other missionaries went northwards, but before long the Danes drove out both their king Harold and his teacher Ansgar. From Denmark, however, the mission spread to Sweden, and in 831 an archbishopric was established at Hamburg to direct all the northern

The
conversion
of the
Danes

K

missions, and Ansgar was invested with the pallium by Pope Gregory IV. The missions had a chequered career. Hamburg was seized and pillaged by the Northmen in 845, and the Swedish mission was for a time destroyed. In 849 a new revival took place, when Ansgar was given the see of Bremen in addition to that of Hamburg; and before long he won over the king of the Jutes and his people of Schleswig. In 853 Ansgar returned to Sweden, where he was favourably received by the king Olaf. The tale of his vast missionary labours, from which he was rightly called the "Apostle of the north," is told with spirit and feeling by Adam of Bremen, who wrote in the eleventh century, as well as by the biographer who commemorated him on his death. He not only preached, but he "redeemed captives, nourished those who were in tribulation, taught his household. As an apostle without, a monk within, he was never idle." When it was said that his prayers wrought miracles of healing, he said, "If I could but think myself worthy of such a favour from the Lord, I would pray Him to grant me but one miracle—that out of me, by His grace, He would make a good man." S. Ansgar is, in his work as in his training, a parallel to S. Boniface. Like him one of the finest fruits of monasticism, which first taught in solitude and then sent out to work actively in the world, he was brought up at Corbie. For nearly thirty-five years he laboured incessantly among the peoples of the north, and at the very end of his life he gallantly went among heathen chiefs to rebuke them for buying and selling slaves. He died in 865, and S. Rimbert,

and of Sweden.

S. Ansgar.

his disciple and biographer, was his successor in his sees.

Gradually, and in different ways, Christianity spread in the far north. Haakon, the son of Harold Haarfager of Norway, was sent to be foster-son to Æthelstan of England, who "had him **Norway.** baptized and brought up in the right faith," and he became a great king under the name of Haakon the Good. From England he brought over teachers, and he built churches; and then at last he addressed all the leaders of his people and besought them "all, young and old, rich and poor, women as well as men, that they should all allow themselves to be baptized, and should believe in one God, and in Christ the Son of Mary, and refrain from all sacrifices and heathen gods, and should keep holy the seventh day, and abstain from all work on it, and keep a fast on the seventh day."[1] But it was long before his people obeyed him. Rebellion and dynastic war followed in rapid succession; and he died of a wound from a chance arrow that struck him as he pursued his defeated foes. The first Christian king of Norway died in a land which was still heathen. But the seed was sown in the hearts of the men who had seen the brave, strong, chivalrous life of him who owned Christ for Lord.

In Denmark the conversion begun in the ninth century was long delayed, and it was not till Otto I. conquered the Danes and sent Bishop Poppo **Olaf** who instructed King Harold and his army **Trigva-** so that they were baptized, that the land **son.**

[1] The Saturday fast was still observed in many parts of Christendom.

became definitely a Christian kingdom. From Denmark the gospel spread again to Norway; but it was not till near the end of the tenth century that Olaf Trigvason was baptized by a hermit on one of the Scilly Isles, and then in his short reign devoted himself to converting his people, often forcibly, as a choice between death and baptism. To Iceland and Greenland too Olaf sent missionaries. He died at last, like a true Wiking hero, in a sea fight; and it was not until the next century and the days of Olaf the Saint that the faith of Christ conquered the North.

There seems no doubt that Christianity in Iceland began by missionary enterprise from Irish monks. The conversion of Iceland. From time to time anchorites sought refuge in that *ultima Thule*, "that they might pray to God in peace"; but whether they did any direct work of conversion is doubtful. The actual conversion came undoubtedly from Norway. A Christian queen lived in Iceland at the end of the ninth century, the wife of the Norse Olaf who was king in Dublin; but little if any impression was made on the heathenism of the people. Nearly a century later an Icelander called Thorwald Kothransson brought a Christian bishop Frederic from Saxony, who wrought some conversions and left a body of baptized Christians behind him. In the year 1000 came a priest Thormod and several chiefs back from the Norse court of Olaf, and in a meeting of the Althing—the great assembly of the people—preached to them the One God in Trinity. The whole people became Christian, and the few heathen customs that still lingered, as it were by permission, after the great baptism, soon fell away like raindrops in the bright sun. Among the last news that came to Olaf Trigvason was that his distant people had fulfilled the wish of his heart.

CHAPTER XII

PROGRESS OF THE CHURCH IN GERMANY

THE acceptance of Christianity and of Catholicism by the barbarian tribes which conquered Europe was a slow process. The conversion of the Lombards, for example, whom we have seen as Arians, sometimes tolerant, sometimes persecuting, was gradual. The Church always held its own, in faith though not in possessions, in Italy; and from the pontificate of Gregory the Great the moral force of the Catholic Society began to win the Lombards to its fold. It was proved again and again that heresy was not a unifying power. The Catholic Church held together its disciples in the Catholic creed. It is possible that Agilulf, the husband of the famous Catholic queen Theodelind, himself became a Catholic before he died. Paul the Deacon says that he "both held the Catholic faith and bestowed many possessions on the Church of Christ, and restored the bishops, who were in a depressed and abject condition, to the honour of their wonted dignity." Whatever may be the meaning of this, it certainly expresses the fact that before the middle of the seventh century the Lombards were passing almost insensibly into the Catholic fold, and Italy had practically become united in one faith though far from united in one government.

With Germany it was different. As the Merwing kingdoms decayed, the Eastern one, Austrasia, with its capital, Metz, was but a poor bulwark against heathen tribes on its borders, which were yet, it might seem at times, little more barbarous than itself. The kingdom of Austrasia stretched eastwards from Rheims "spreading across the Rhine an unknown distance into Germany, claiming the allegiance of Thuringians, Alamanni and Bavarians, fitfully controlling the restless Saxons, touching with warlike weapons and sometimes vainly striving with the terrible Avars." [1] Kings of the Bavarian line came to rule in Northern Italy, but Bavaria was little touched by Christian faith. At last when the descendants of Arnulf [2] came as kings over a now again united Frankish monarchy, when Charles Martel made one power of Austrasia, Neustria, and Burgundy, the time for a new advance seemed to have come. Theodelind, the Catholic queen of the Lombards, was herself of Bavarian birth, but a century after her time the people of her native land, it seems, were still heathen. They were apart from the Roman civilisation and the Catholic tradition: conversion, to touch them, must be a direct and aggressive movement.

The Church in the Frankish kingdoms.

At the end of the seventh century S. Rupert began the work. He settled his episcopal throne at Salzburg. He was followed by Emmeran, and by Corbinian. Slowly the work proceeded, hindered by violence on the part of dukes and saints, favoured by popes and making a beginning for Roman missionary interest in the distant borders of the Empire under the Germans.

[1] Hodgkin, *Italy and her Invaders*, v. 203.
[2] See p. 144.

But it was not to these Frankish missionaries, or to Roman envoys, that the most important work was due. It was due to an outburst of converting zeal on the part of the newly converted race who had made Britain the land of the English.

Of all the great missionaries of the eighth century perhaps the greatest was Winfrith of Crediton, an Englishman who became the father of German Christianity and the precursor of the great religious and intellectual movement of the days of Charles the Great. He followed the Northumbrian Willibrord who for twenty-six years had laboured in Frisia, and supported by the commission of Gregory II. he set forth in 719 to preach to the fierce heathens of Germany. He was instructed to use the Roman rite and to report to Rome any difficulties he might encounter. He began to labour in Thuringia, a land where Irish missionaries had already been at work, and where he recalled the Christians from evil ways into which they had lapsed. He passed on through Neustria and thence to Frisia, where for three years he "laboured much in Christ, converting not a few, destroying the heathen shrines and building Christian oratories," aiding the venerable Willibrord in the work he had so long carried on. But he felt the call to labour in lands as yet untouched, and so he determined to go to the Germans. As he passed up the Rhine he drew to him the boy Gregory afterwards famous as abbat of Utrecht, and at last he settled in the forests of Hessen and built a monastery at Amöneburg. From his old friends in England he received sound advice as to the treatment of heathen customs and the gentle methods of conversion which befit the gospel of

Saint Boniface.

Christ. From Rome he received affectionate support ; and in 722 he was summoned to receive a new mission from the pope himself. On S. Andrew's Day,723,[1] after a solemn profession of faith in the Holy Trinity and of obedience to the Roman See—the first ever taken by one outside the Roman patriarchate—he was consecrated bishop. He set out with letters from the pope to Christians of Thuringia and to the duke Charles. Charles Martel accepted the trust and gave to Winfrith (who had assumed the name of Boniface) the pledge of his protection. The missionary's first act on his return to Hessen was to destroy the ancient oak at Geismar, the object of devotion to the worshippers of the Germanic gods; and the act was followed by many conversions of those who saw that heathenism could not resent the attack upon its sacred things. Still there were difficulties. Those who had learned from the old Celtic mission were not ready to accept the Roman customs. Gregory II. wrote in 724, exhorting him to perseverance : " Let not threats alarm thee, nor terrors cast thee down, but stayed in confidence on God proclaim the word of truth. The work grew : monasteries and churches arose : many English helpers came over : the favour of Charles Martel was a protection. As the Benedictines opened out new lands, ploughed, built, studied, taught, religion and education spread before him. In 732 Boniface was made archbishop, received a pallium from Rome, and was encouraged by the new pope Gregory III. to organise the Church which he had founded and

His mission from Rome, 723.

Boniface archbishop 732.

---

[1] This seems to me the most probable date. Cf. Hauck, *Kirchengeschichte Deutschlands*, i. 448.

to spread forth his arms into the land of the Bavarians.
There Christianity had already made some way under
Frankish missionaries : it needed organisation from the
hand of a master.   He " exercised himself diligently,"
says his biographer Willibald, "in preaching, and went
round inspecting many churches."   In 738 he paid his
last visit to Rome, where he stayed nearly a year and
was treated with extraordinary respect and affection.
On his return he divided Bavaria into the four dioceses
of Salzburg, Regensburg, Freising, and Passau, and later
on he founded other sees also, including Würzburg.   It
was his next aim to do something to reform the lax
morals of the Frankish Church, which had sunk to a
low ebb under the Merwings.   The Austrasian Synod,
which bears in some respects a close resemblance to
the almost contemporary English Synod of Clovesho
(747), of 742 dealt boldly with these matters.   Other
councils followed in which Boniface took a leading
His mis- part, and which made a striking reforma-
sionary tion.   His equally important work was to
work and complete the conquest of the general spirit
martyrdom. of Western Christendom, which looked to
Rome for leadership, over the Celtic missionaries,
noble missionaries and martyrs who yet lacked the
instinct of cohesion and solidarity.   A long series of
letters, to the popes, to bishops, princes and persons of
importance, shows the breadth of his interests and the
nature of his activity.   To " four peoples," he says, he
had preached the gospel, the Hessians, Thuringians,
Franks and Bavarians, not to all for the first time but
as a reformer and one who removed heathen influences
from the Church.   As Archbishop of Mainz he was
untiring even in advanced age : in politics as well as in

religion he was a leader of men. It was he who anointed Pippin at Soissons in 751 and thus gave the Church's sanction to the new Karling line. He determined to end his days as a missionary to the heathen. In 755 he went with a band of priests and monks once more to the wild Frisians, and at Dokkum by the northern sea he met his death at the hands of the heathen whom he came to win to Christ. The day, ever remembered, was June 5, 755.

Boniface was truly attached to the popes, truly respectful to the Roman See: but he preserved his independence. His attitude towards the secular power was precisely similar. He was a great churchman, a great statesman, a great missionary; but his religious and political opinions cannot be tied down to the limits of some strict theory. His was a wide, genial nature, in things spiritual and in things temporal genuine, sincere; a true Saint, a true Apostle. Through the lives and sacrifices of such men it was that the Church came to exercise so profound an influence over the politics of the Middle Age.

The work which S. Boniface began was continued by weapons other than his own. When the Empire of the Romans was revived (as we shall tell in the next chapter) by the chiefs of the Arnulf house, when a Catholic Cæsar was again acclaimed in the Roman churches, the ideas on which the new monarchy was to rest were decisively Christian and Catholic. Charles the son of Pippin was a student of theology, among many other things. He believed firmly that it was a real kingdom of God which he was called to form and govern upon earth. The spirit which inspired the followers of

The Emperors and missions.

Muhammad inspired him too. He was determined
not to leave to priests and popes the propagation of
the faith which he believed.

For thirty-two years Charles the Great, as his
people came to call him, was engaged in a war which
Charles claimed to be waged for the spread of the
and the Christian faith. Charles was before all
Saxons. things in belief (though not always in life)
a Christian, and it was intolerable to him that within
the German lands should remain a large and powerful
body of heathens. In 772 he marched into the land
of the Angarii and destroyed the Irminsul, a column
which was representative of the power which the
Saxons worshipped. It was destroyed, and the army
after its victories returned in triumph. In 774 the
Saxons turned the tables and burnt the abbey of
Fritzlar which had been founded by S. Boniface. In
775 Charles resolved to avenge this loss, but made
little progress. In 776 he was more successful, and
a great multitude of Saxons submitted and were
baptized. In 777 there was another great baptism,
but, says the chronicler, the Saxons were perfidious.
In 778 when Charles was in Spain the Saxons de-
vastated a vast tract of land, and even for a time stole
the body of S. Boniface from its tomb at Fulda. Charles
crushed the resistance, and from 780 he set himself
to organise the Church in the Saxon lands, issuing
severe edicts which practically enforced Christianity
on the conquered Saxons with the penalty of death
for the performance of pagan rites, and even for eating
meat in Lent. A law was also decreed that all men
should give a tenth of their substance and work to
the churches and priests. Still the conquest was not

durable, for a terrible insurrection in 782 slew a whole army of the Germans and massacred priests and monks wherever they could be found. Then came years of carnage: once Charles—it is said—caused 4,500 Saxons to be beheaded in one day. In 793 there was a new outbreak. The Saxons "as a dog returneth to his vomit so returned they to the pagan- ism they had renounced, again deserting Christian faith and lying not less to God than to their lord the king." Churches were destroyed, bishops and priests slain, and the land was again defiled with blood. They allied with the Avars, and Charles was thus beset with heathen foes in Hungary and in North Germany at once. He tried every measure of devasta- tion and exile; but it seems that by 797 he had come more clearly to see the Christian way. " Let but the same pains be taken," he wrote—or the English scholar Alcuin wrote for him—" to preach the easy yoke and light burden of Christ to the obstinate people of the Saxons as are taken to collect the tithes from them or to punish the least transgression of the laws imposed on them, and perhaps they would be found no longer to repel baptism with abhorrence." But he was far from always acting up to this view, and he even allied with heathen Slavs to accomplish the subjugation of his enemies. As he conquered he mapped out the land in bishoprics and planted monasteries at im- portant points: he took Saxon boys to his court and sent them back trained, often as ecclesiastics, to teach and rule. Among such was Ebbo, afterwards Archbishop of Rheims, the "Apostle of Denmark." From abroad too came other missionaries, and notable among them was another Englishman, Willehad of

Northumbria, who became in 788 the first bishop of Bremen. At last Christianity was, at least nominally, in possession from the Rhine to the Elbe, and in the words of Einhard "thus they were brought to accept the terms of the king, and thus they gave up their demon worship, renounced their national religious customs, embraced the Christian faith, received the divine sacraments, and were united with the Franks, forming one people."

Under Charles the organisation of the German Church, begun by Boniface, received a great extension. It was possible, after his death, to regard Germany as Christian and as organised in its religion on the lines of all the Western Churches.

CHAPTER XIII

THE POPES

AND THE REVIVAL OF THE EMPIRE

THE growth of the temporal power of the bishops of
Rome was due to two causes, the withdrawal of
the imperial authority from Italy and the conversion
of the barbarians. As the emperors at Constantinople
became more and more busied with affairs   Growth of
Eastern, with the encroachments of bar-   papal
barians, heathen and Muhammadan, and   power.
the imperial rule in Italy was destroyed by the Lombards, the popes stood out as the one permanent
institution in Northern and Central Italy. As gradually the barbarians came to accept the faith they
received it at the hands of the great ecclesiastical
organisation which kept together the traditions, so
strangely transformed, of the Old Rome. The legislation of Justinian also had given great political power
to the popes: and this power was greatly increased
when the papacy found itself the leader in the resistance
of the great majority of Christian peoples against the
policy of the Iconoclastic emperors. The history of
Rome began to run on very different lines from that of
Venice, Naples, or other great cities. It became for a
while a conflict between the local military nobility
and the clergy under the rule of the pope. The

143

struggle was a political one, just as the assumption of
power by the popes, of power over the country and a
considerable district around it, was a political act.

The popes had but very slight relations with the
kings of the Merwing house. It was different when
the Karlings came into power. Zacharias, both directly
and through S. Boniface, came into close connection
with Pippin and Carloman. At first he was concerned
simply with reform in the Frankish Church, but before
long he found himself able to intervene in a critical
event and to take part in the inauguration of the
Karling House, the revival as it claimed to be of the
Empire in the West.

The growth of the papal power was closely associated
with two other historic events : the growth of the
Karling house among the Franks, and the
process of revival in the Church's spiritual
activity, showing itself in missions without
and reforms within. The last leads back to the first.

The Kar-
ling refor-
mation.

Whatever may be thought of the Karling reformation,
it cannot be denied that for the century before Charles
assumed the Imperial crown the Church showed many
signs of corruption. The darkness of the picture is
relieved only by the lives of some remarkable saints.

The first, of course, is S. Arnulf, Bishop of Metz, the
great-grandfather of Charles Martel. Born about 582,
he died in 641, and the holy simplicity
of his life as statesman and priest comes
like a ray of sunshine in the gloom of the
days of " half heathen and wholly vicious " kings. Mr.
Hodgkin, with an eye no doubt to modern affairs, com-
ments thus on the career of the prelate so different
from the greedy, turbulent, and licentious men whom

The
Karling
House.

Gregory of Tours describes: "In reading his life one cannot but feel that in some way the Frankish nation, or at least the Austrasian part of it, has groped its way upwards since the sixth century." Arnulf was a type of the good bishops of the Middle Ages, strong, able to hold his own with kings, a friend of the poor, eager to pass from the world to a quiet eventide in some monastic shade. The tale that is told of him is typical of the sympa- thies and passions of his age. Bishop of Metz, and chief counsellor of Dagobert whose father Chlothochar he had helped to raise to the throne, when he ex- pressed his wish to retire from the world the king cried out that if he did he would slay his two sons. "My sons' lives are in the hands of God," said Arnulf. "Yours will not last long if you slay the innocent"; and when Dagobert drew his sword on him he said, "Would you return good for evil ? Here am I ready to die in obedience to Him Who gave me life and Who died for me." Queen and nobles cried out, and the king fell penitent at the bishop's feet. Like S. Arnulf's is the romantic figure of his descendant Carloman, who turned from the rule of kingdoms and the command of armies to the seclusion of Soracte and Monte Cassino. The "great renunciation" is a striking tale. The dis- appearance of the long days of patient submission to rule, the discovery of the real position of the humble brother, and then the last dramatic appearance to follow an unpopular cause, make a story as striking as any which have come to us from the Middle Age. But before Carloman come many other noble figures. The fifty years that followed Arnulf's death are but a dreary tale of anarchy and blood. It is broken here and there

S. Arnulf.

L

by records of Christian endurance or martyrdom: bishops who tried to serve the State often served not wisely but too well and met the fate of unsuccessful political leaders. Leodegar, Bishop of Autun, who helped Ebroin to raise Theoderic III. to the throne of Neustria, was blinded, imprisoned and at length put to death and appears in the Church's calendar as S. Leger.

The crisis came when the long march of the successful Muhammadans was stayed by the arms of S. Arnulf's descendant Charles Martel, mayor of the palace to the King of Austrasia 717, to all the kingdoms from 719, who lived till 741. In 711 the Wisigothic monarchy of Spain had fallen before the infidels: in 720 the Moors entered Gaul. From then to 731 there was for Abder Rahman an almost unbroken triumph. The power of the Prophet reached from Damascus to beyond the Pyrenees. Then Charles Martel came to the relief of Southern Gaul, and on an October Sunday in 732 the hosts of Islam were utterly routed at Poictiers by the soldiers of the Cross. It was a great deliverance; **The defeat of the Saracens.** and there is no wonder that imagination has exaggerated its importance and thought that but for the Moorish defeat there might to-day be a muezzin in every Highland steeple and an Imám set over every Oxford college. Charles had still to reconquer Septimania and Provence. Arles and Nîmes, the great Roman cities, had to be recovered from the Arabs who had seized them, and Avignon, Agde, Béziers, cities whose future was as wonderful as was the others' past, were also won back by the arms of the Christian chief.

Charles died in 741. He had refused to help Pope

Gregory III. in 739 against the Lombards. It was reserved for his son Pippin to make that alliance between
the papacy and the Karling house which dictated the
future of Europe. To Pippin came the lordship of the
West Franks, to Carloman his brother that   Pippin.
of the East Franks, when their father died.
They conquered, they reformed the Church among the
Franks, with the aid of Boniface, and then came that
dramatic retirement of Carloman in 747 which showed
him to be true heir of S. Arnulf. Four years later the
house of the Karlings became the nominal as well as
the real rulers of the Franks. In 751 the bishop of
Würzburg for the East Franks, and the abbat of S. Denis
for those of the West, went to Rome to ask the pope's
advice. Were the wretched Merwings " who were of
royal race and were called kings but had no power in
the realm save that grants and charters were drawn up
in their names " to be still called kings, for " what
willed the *major domus* of the Franks, that they did? "
Zacharias answered as a wise man would, that he who
had the power should bear the name. And so, blessed
by the great missionary S. Boniface, Pippin was
" heaved " on the shield, and became king of the
Franks, and Childerich, the last of the Merwings,
went to a distant monastery to end his days.

But this was only a beginning. The pope was
threatened by the barbarians, neglected by the
emperors who reigned at Constantinople,   The end
and at last was in actual conflict with those   of the
who tried to impose Iconoclasm upon the   Imperial
Church. In 751 the exarchate, the repre-   power in
sentation of the Imperial power in Italy,   Italy.
with its seat at Ravenna, was overwhelmed by the

arms of Aistulf, the Lombard king. The time had
come, thought Pope Stephen II. (752–7), when the
distant barbarians, now orthodox, should be called to
save the patrimony of S. Peter from the barbarians
near at hand. In S. Peter's name letters summoned
Pippin to the rescue of the church especially dear to
the Franks.[1] But before this Stephen had made
Pippin his friend. In 753 he left Rome and failing
to win from Aistulf any concession to the Imperial
power made his way across the Alps, and on the Feast
of the Epiphany, 754, met in their own land Pippin
and his son who was to be Charles the Great. The
pope fell at the king's feet and besought him by the
mercies of God to save the Romans from the hands of
the Lombards. Then Pippin and all his lords held up
their hands in sign of welcome and support. Then
Stephen on July 28, 754, in the great monastery
which was to become the crowning-place of Frankish
kings, anointed Pippin and his sons Charles and
Carloman as king of the Franks and kings in
succession.

A point of special interest in this event is the
title given to Pippin at his crowning at Saint Denis.
The crown-
ing of
Pippin.
The title of Patrician of the Romans was
given by the pope, as commissioned by the
emperor, "to act against the king of the
Lombards for the recovery of the lost lands of the
Empire." Pippin was made the officer of the distant
emperor, and the pope would say as little as possible
about the rights of him who ruled in Constantinople,
and as much as he could about the Church which
ruled in Rome. It was a step in the assertion of

[1] *Cod. Car.* in Muratori, *Rer. Ital. Script.*, iii. (2) 96.

political rights for the Roman Church. A new order of things was springing up in Italy. The popes were asserting a political power as belonging to S. Peter. They were asserting that the exarchate had ceased in political theory as well as in practical fact. In this new order Pippin was to be involved as supporter of the protectorate which the papacy assumed to itself.

Then the Franks came forward to save Rome from the Lombards. The last act of the romantic life of Carloman was to plead for justice to Aistulf,—that what he had won should not be taken from him,—and to be refused. Twice Pippin came south and saved the pope: and then the cities he had won he refused to give up to the envoys of the distant emperor and declared that "never should those cities be alienated from the power of S. Peter and the rights of the Roman Church and the pontiff of the Apostolic See." From this dates the Roman pope's independence of the Roman emperor, the definite political severance of Italy from the East, and therefore a great step towards the schism of the Church. Iconoclasm and the independence of the popes alike worked against the unity of Christendom.

Pope Stephen, thanks to Pippin, had become the arbitrator of Italy. The keys of Ravenna and of the twenty-two cities which "stretched along the Adriatic coast from the mouths of the Po to within a few miles of Ancona and inland as far as the Apennines" were laid on the tomb of S. Peter. The "States of the Church" began their long history, the history of "the temporal power."

And this new power was seen outside Italy as well

The papal power.

as within. From the eighth century, at least, the popes are found continually intervening in the affairs of the churches among the Franks and the Germans, granting privileges, giving indulgence, writing with explicit claim to the authority which Christ gave to S. Peter. Into the recesses of Gaul, among Normans at Rouen, among Lotharingians at Metz, to Amiens, or Venice, or Limoges, the papal letters penetrated; and their tone is that of confidence that advice will be respected or commands obeyed. And this is in small matters especially, rather than in great. The popes at least claimed to interfere everywhere in Christian Europe and in everything.[1] Within Italy events moved quickly.

The first step towards a new development was the destruction of the Lombard kingdom by Charles, who succeeded his father Pippin in 768. At first joint ruler with his brother he became on the latter's death in 771 sole king of all the Franks. In 772 Hadrian I., a Roman, ambitious and distinguished, succeeded the weak Stephen III. on the papal throne. He reigned till 795 and one of his first acts was to summon Charles **Charles** and the Franks to his rescue against the **the Great** Lombards. In the midst of his conquests— **and Rome.** which it is not here our part to tell—Charles spent the Holy Week and Easter of 774 at Rome. Thus the one contemporary authority tells the tale of the great alliance which was made on the Wednesday in Easter week: " On the fourth day of the week the aforesaid pontiff with all his nobles both clerkly and knightly went forth to S. Peter's Church and there

[1] Cf. Dr. J. von Pflugk-Hartung, *Acta Pontificum Romanorum inedita*, 1880, 1884.

meeting the king in colloquy earnestly prayed him and with paternal affection admonished him to fulfil entirely that promise which his father of holy memory the dead king Pippin had made, and which he himself with his brother Carloman and all the nobles of the Franks had confirmed to S. Peter and his vicar Pope Stephen II. of holy memory when he visited Francia, that they would grant divers cities and territories in that province of Italy to S. Peter and his vicars for ever. And when Charles had caused the promise which was made in Francia at a place called Carisiacum (Quierzy) to be read over to him all its contents were approved by him and his nobles. And of his will and with a good and gracious mind that most excellent and most Christian king Charles caused another promise of gift like the first to be drawn up by Etherius his most religious and prudent chaplain and notary, and in this he gave the same cities and lands to S. Peter and promised that they should be handed over to the pope with their boundaries set forth as is contained in the aforesaid donation, namely: From Luna with the island of Corsica, thence to Surianum, thence to Mount Bardo, that is to Vercetum, thence to Parma, thence to Rhegium, and from thence to Mantua and Mons Silicis, together with the whole exarchate of Ravenna, as it was of old, and the provinces of the Venetia and Istria; together with the whole duchy of Spoletium and that of Beneventum.[1] The donation was confirmed, says the chronicler, with the most solemn oaths.

Now if this records the facts, and if two-thirds of Italy were given by Charles (who possessed very little

[1] *Liber Pontificalis*, i. 498.

of it) to the popes, it is almost incredible that his later
conduct should have shown that he did not pay any
regard to it. But the question is of political rather
than ecclesiastical interest, and it may suffice to say
that there are very strong reasons for believing the
passage to be a later interpolation.[1]

Within four months Charles had subdued the Lombards and become "rex Francorum et Langobardorum

**The revival
of the
Empire,
800.**
atque patricius Romanorum." For nearly
a quarter of a century Charles was employed
in other parts of his empire: he dealt
friendly but firmly with the pope; but he
kept away from Rome. But in 799 the new pope
Leo III., attacked by the Romans probably for some
harshness in his rule, fled from the city and in July
came to Charles at Paderborn to entreat his help. It
is probable that the great English scholar, Alcuin,
who has been called the Erasmus of the eighth
century, had already suggested to the great king that
the weakness of the Eastern emperors was a real
defeasance of power and that the crown imperial
might be his own. However that may be Charles
came to Rome and made a triumphal entry on November 24, 800. The charges against the pope were heard
and he swore to his innocence. On the feast of the
Nativity, in the basilica of S. Peter, when Charles had
worshipped at the *confessio,* the tomb of S. Peter, Leo
clothed him with a purple robe and set a crown of gold
upon his head. "Then all the faithful Romans behold-
ing so great a champion given them and the love which

---

[1] The question may be read in Mgr. Duchesne's Introduction to
the *Liber Pontificalis,* ccxxxvii.–ccxlii ; and Dr. Hodgkin, *Italy
and her Invaders,* vii. 387–97.

he bore towards the holy Roman Church and its vicar, in obedience to the will of God and S. Peter the key-bearer of the kingdom of heaven, cried with one accord in sound like thunder 'To Charles the most pious Augustus, crowned of God, the Emperor great and peaceable, life and victory!'"

Thus the Roman pope and the Roman people claimed to make anew in Rome the Roman Empire with a German for Cæsar and Augustus. It was not, if we believe Charles's own close friend Einhard, a distinction sought by the new emperor himself. "At first he so disliked the title of *Imperator* and *Augustus* that he declared that if he had known before the intention of the pope he would never have entered the church on that day, though it was one of the most holy festivals of the year."[1] It may well be that Charles, who had corresponded with the Cæsars of the East, hesitated to take a step of such bold defiance. Men still preserved the memories of how the soldiers of Justinian had won back Italy from the Goths. Nor was Charles pleased to receive such a gift at the hands of the pope. He did not recognise the right of a Roman pontiff to give away the imperial crown. What could be given could be taken away. It was a precedent of evil omen.

But none the less the coronation of Charles the Great, as men came to call him, was the greatest event in the Middle Age. It showed the vitality of the idea of empire which the West inherited from the Romans, and it showed that idea linked to the new power of the popes. It founded the Holy Roman Empire. Twelve years later the Empire of the West won some sort of recognition from the Empire of the East. In 812 an ambassage from Constantinople came

[1] *Liber Pontificalis*, ii. 6.

to Charles at Aachen, and Charles was hailed by them as Imperator and Basileus. The Empire of the West was an accomplished and recognised fact.

Its significance was at least as much religious as political. Charles delighted in the works of S. Augustine and most of all in the *De Civitate Dei*; and that great book is the ideal of a Christian State, which shall be Church and State together, and which replaces the Empire of pagan Rome. The abiding idea of unity had been preserved by the Church : it was now to be strengthened by the support of a head of the State. The one Christian commonwealth was to be linked together in the bond of divine love under one emperor and one pope. That Constantine the first Christian emperor had given to the popes the sovereignty of the West was a fiction which it seems was already known at Rome : Hadrian seems to have referred to the strange fable when he wrote to Charles the Great in 777. It was a legend very likely of Eastern fabrication, and it was probably not as yet believed to have any claim to be authentic ; but when the papacy had grown great at the expense of the Empire it was to be a powerful weapon in the armoury of the popes. Now it served only, with the revival of learning at the court of Charles the Great, to illustrate two sides of the great movement for the union of Europe under two monarchs, the spiritual and the temporal. The coronation of Charles was indeed a fact the importance of which, as well as the conflicts which would inevitably flow from it, lay in the future. But it showed the Roman Church great, and it showed the absorption of the great Teutonic race in the fascinating ideal of unity at once Christian and imperial.

Results of the revived Empire.

CHAPTER XIV

THE ICONOCLASTIC CONTROVERSY

WE have spoken already of two important periods in the history of the Eastern Church. We must now briefly sketch another.

The third period (725-847) is that of Iconoclasm. Of this, the originator was the emperor Leo III., one of those soldiers who endeavour to apply to   Sketch of the sanctuary the methods of the parade- the period, ground. He issued a decree against the 725-847. reverence paid to icons (religious images and pictures), and, in 729, replaced the patriarch S. Germanus by the more supple Anastasius; a docile assembly of bishops at Hieria, under Constantine V. (Copronymus), passed a decree against every image of the Lord, the Virgin, and the saints. A fierce persecution followed, which was hardly ended before the accession to power of Irene, widow of Leo IV., under whom assembled the Seventh General Council at Nicæa in 787, a Council to which the West and .the distant East sent representatives. This Council decreed that icons should be used and receive veneration ($\pi\rho\sigma\sigma\kappa\acute{\nu}\nu\eta\sigma\iota\varsigma$) as did the Cross and the book of the Gospels. A persecution followed, as bitter as that of the iconoclastic emperors, and the troubled years of the first half of the ninth century, stained in Byzantium by every crime, found almost their only brightness in the patriarchate (843-7) of S. Methodius, a wise ruler, an orthodox theologian, a charitable man. In Antioch and Jerusalem, about the same period, orthodox patriarchs were re-established by the toleration of the Ommeyads and the earlier Abbassides; but on the European frontiers of the Empire conversion was at a standstill during the whole period of iconoclastic fury and reaction, while in the north-east of Syria and in Armenia the heresy of the Paulicians (Adoptianism) spread and flourished, and the Monophysites still throve on the Asiatic borders. In theology the Church of Constantinople was still strong, as is shown by the great work of S. Theodore of the Studium, famous as a hymn-writer, a liturgiologist, and a defender of the faith.

Such are the facts, briefly summarised, of the history of rather more than a century in the East. But we must examine more attentively the meaning of the great strife which divided the Eastern Church.

The orthodox doctrine, as it is now defined, is this— that " the icons are likenesses engraved or painted in

The orthodox doctrine of images.
oil on wood or stone or any sort of metal, of our Saviour Christ, of the Mother of God, and of the holy men who from Adam have been well-pleasing to God. From earliest times the icons have been used not only to give internal dignity and beauty to every Christian church and house, but, which is much more essential, for the instruction and moral education of Christians. For when any Christian looks at the icons, he at once recalls the life and deeds of those who are represented upon them, and desires to conform himself to their example. On this account also the Church decreed in early times that due reverence should always be paid

by Christians to the holy icons, which honour of course is not rendered to the picture before our eyes, but to the original of the picture." This statement represents the views of the orthodox Eastern theologians of the eighth as clearly as it does the teaching of the nineteenth century. It represents also the opinions of the popes contemporary with the Iconoclastic movement, who withstood the emperors to the face. Leo was threatened by Gregory II., and the patriarch who had yielded to the storm, Anastasius, was excommunicated. The pope advocated, in clear dogmatic language, the use of images for instruction of the ignorant and encouragement of the faithful. In Greece there was something like a revolution, but it was sternly repressed. In 731 a council, at which the archbishops of Ravenna and Grado were present, and ninety-three other Italian prelates, with a large representation of the laity, under Pope Gregory III., ordered that if anyone should stand forth as "a destroyer, profaner, and blasphemer against the veneration of the holy images, that is of Christ and His sinless Mother, of the blessed Apostles and the Saints, he should be excluded from the body and blood of Jesus Christ, and from all the unity and fabric of the Church." The answer to this, it would seem, was the separation of the Illyrian territories and sees from the Roman patriarchate, as well as the sees in Sicily and Calabria : the pope's authority was restricted to the territory of the exarchate, including Rome, Venice and Ravenna. In Constantinople the resistance of the people to the Iconoclastic decrees was met by a bitter persecution, which Constantine V. began in 761. Under

The accept-
ance in
the West.

his father Leo III. the virgin Theodosia was martyred,

The Iconoclastic persecution. who is revered among the most popular of the Saints in Constantinople to-day. The position of the people who clung to their old ways of worship in the eighth century was indeed not unlike that of those who to-day struggle on, always in dread of active persecution, under the Muhammadan rule. Muhammadanism, with its stern suppression of all representation of things divine or human, was believed to have been one of the suggesting forces which brought about the Iconoclastic movement. Leo III. had been brought into intimate association with the Saracens; and it was said in his own day that he had learned his fury against images from one of them. The tale was a fable, but it showed how entirely Leo's action was contrary to the religious feeling of his time.

It is difficult perhaps for a Western, or at least an Anglican, to-day to form a just estimate of the **Iconoclastic theology.** strong feeling of the majority of the Eastern Christians in favour of "image-worship." It is easy to see how the stern simplicity of the Muhammadan worship, which in all the strength of the creed that carried its disciples in triumphant march over continents and over ancient civilisations was present to the eyes of the soldiers of Heraclius and Leo, appealed to all those who knew the power and the need of stern self-restraint. That Islam should seem to be more spiritual than Christianity seemed irony indeed, but an irony which seemed to have facts to prove it. An age of superstition, an age of credulous hunts after the miraculous, an age when materialism made rapid progress among

THE ICONOCLASTIC CONTROVERSY

the courtiers of the great city, was an age, it might well seem, which needed a protest against "icono-duly," as the iconoclasts termed the custom of the Eastern Church. And if the controversy could have been kept away from the field of pure theology it might well have been that an Iconoclastic victory would not have been other than a benefit to religion. Leo was content to replace the crucifix by a cross. But it is impossible to sunder the symbol from the doctrine, and the Greeks would never rest satisfied with a defini-tion, still less with a practical change, without probing to its inner meaning. This feeling was expressed in form philosophical and theological by one of the last of the great Greek Fathers, S. John Damascene, and by the united voice of the Church in the decision of the Seventh General Council.

S. John of Damascus, who died about 760, was clear in his acceptance of all the Councils of the Church, clear in his rejection of Monophysitism and Monothelitism. He described in clear pre-cision the two natures in one hypostasis, the two wills, human and Divine, with a wisdom and knowledge related to each; but he was equally clear that the composite personality involves a *communi-catio idiomatum* (ἀντίδοσις ἰδιωμάτων). The human nature taken up into the Divine received the glory of the Divinity: the Divine "imparts to the human nature of its own glories, remaining itself impas-sible and without share in the passions of humanity." S. John Damascene taught then that our Lord's humanity was so enriched by the Divine Word as to know the future, though this knowledge was only manifested progressively as He increased in age, and

S. John Damas-cene.

that only for our sakes did He progressively manifest
His knowledge. While he declared that each Nature
in the Divine Person had its will, he explained that
the One Person directed both, and that His Divine will
was the determinant will. It might well seem that
in his desire to avoid Nestorianism he did not attach
so full a meaning to our Lord's advance in human
knowledge as did some of the earlier Fathers. But
the practical bearing of S. John's writings was in
direct relation to the great controversy of his age,
to which he devoted three addresses in particular.
He defined the "worship" of the icons as all based
upon the worship of Christ, and attacked iconoclasm
as involving ultimately an assault upon the doctrine
of the Incarnation. On this ground S. Theodore of
the Studium and Nicephorus the patriarch of Constantinople, who was driven from his see by the
emperor, are at one with S. John Damascene.

Theodore of the Studium occupies a place in Greek
thought which is, perhaps, comparable to that of S.
Anselm in the Latin Church. If there
never was anything in the East exactly
corresponding to the era of the schoolmen
in the West, if the theology of Byzantium throughout might seem to be a scholasticism, but a scholasticism apart, still it would not be untrue to describe
S. Theodore as the last of the Greek Fathers. He
came at a time in Byzantine history when a great
crisis was before the Church and State, so closely
conjoined in the Eastern Empire. Born in the last
half of the eighth century, and dying on November
11th, 826, Theodore lived through the most vital
period of the Iconoclastic struggle, and he left, in his

*S. Theo-
dore of the
Studium.*

theological and familiar writings, the most important memorial of the orthodox position which he did so much to render victorious.

Theodore of the Studium is a striking example of the influence of environment, tradition, and *esprit de corps*. His life is inextricably bound up with the history, and his opinions were indubitably formed to a very large extent by the influence, of the great monastery of S. John Baptist of the Studium, founded towards the close of the fourth century by Fl. Studius, a Roman patrician, the remains of which still charm the traveller who penetrates through the obscurest part of Constantinople to the quarter of Psamatia. The house was dedicated to S. John Baptist, and according to the Russian traveller, Antony of Novgorod, it contained special relics of the Precursor. A later description shows the extreme beauty, seclusion, severity of the place, surrounded by cypress trees and looking forth on the great city which was mistress of the world. Even to-day the splendid columns which still remain and the impressive beauty of the crypt make the church, though in an almost ruinous condition, a striking object in Constantinople. The monastery first became famous as the home of the Akoimetai, or Sleepless Monks, (as they were called from their hours of prayer,) when they withstood the heresies of the later fifth century,[1] and fell themselves into error, but from the date of the Fifth General Council to the outbreak of the Iconoclastic controversy they remained in comparative obscurity.

The era of Iconoclasm, which did so much to devastate the East, and which, by the emigration of some

[1] See above, pp. 8, 14.

50,000 Christians, cleric and lay, to Calabria, exercised
so important an influence on the history of Southern
Italy, might have cast a fatal blight on the Church in
Constantinople had it not been for the stand made by
the Monks of the Studium. The age of the Icono-

The
Monks
of the
Studium
and the
Icono-
clastic
Con-
troversy.

clasts was the golden age of the Studite
monks. Persecuted, expelled from their
house by Constantine Copronymus, they
were restored at his death in 775, but had
dwindled, it seems, to the number of twelve.
A new era of power began for them under
their Archimandrite Sabbas, and this was
increased by his successor, Theodore, whose
life covered the period of the greatest theological
importance in the history of Iconoclasm. When the
patriarchal see was held for seven-and-twenty years
by Iconoclasts, Theodore upheld the spirits of his
brethren, and even in exile contrived to be their
indefatigable leader and support. His was never a
submissive, but always an active resistance to the
imperial attempt to dragoon the Church, and a typical
audacity was the solemn procession with all the
monastery's icons, the monks singing the hymn "Τὴν
ἄχραντον εἰκόνα σοῦ προσκυνοῦμεν, ἀγαθέ," which caused
his expulsion. His exile produced a series of impressive letters in which, with every vigour and
cogency of argument of which a logical Greek was
capable, he exhorted, encouraged, and consoled those
who, like himself, remained steadfast to their faith.
The Studium gave, too, its actual martyrs, James and
Thaddeus, to the traditional belief; and Theodore in
exile, who would gladly have borne them company
in their death, commemorated their heroism and

implored their intercessions. Theodore's whole life was one of resistance, active or passive, to the attempt of the emperors to dictate the Church's Creed; and though he did not live to see the conclusion of the conflict, its final result was largely due to his persistent and strenuous efforts. For a while after his death there is silence over the history of the Studites, till, in 844, we find them bringing back his body in solemn triumph from the island of Prinkipo. Till the middle of the ninth century they remained a potent force; from that time up to the capture of Constantinople by the Turks, if they retained their fame, their activity was diminished.

Professor Marin[1] has collected interesting details from many sources as to the rule of the house, its dress, liturgical customs, learning, discipline. The liturgy was said at six on days when the fast lasted till nine, at three on other days; and the monks were expected to communicate daily. While the house was essentially a learned society, a community of sacred scholars, Theodore stands out from its whole annals as a great preacher, and no less for the charm of his personal character. It was he, fitly, who gave to the house that special Rule, which stood in the same relation to the general customary observance by Eastern monks of that somewhat vague series of laws known as "the Rule of Basil," that the reform of Odo of Cluny stood to the work of S. Benedict himself. It was an eminently sensible codification of floating custom in regard to monastic life. All that Theodore did—and this applies with special force to the sermons which he

The rule of the Studium.

[1] *De Studio Cœnobio Constantinopolitano*, Paris, 1897.

preached—seems to have been eminently practical, charitable, and sane. There is an underlying force of the same kind in the argument of his three *Antirrhetici*, in which he triumphantly vindicates the worship of Christ in His Godhead and His manhood as being inseparable and essential to the true knowledge of the faith as it is in Jesus. There can be no rivalry between icon and prototype: "The worship of the image is worship of Christ, because the image is what it is in virtue of likeness to Christ."

This was the point on which the orthodox met the theologians who defended iconoclasm: the iconoclasts in seeking to destroy all images were seen to strike at a vital truth of the Incarnation, the true humanity of Jesus. The theologians demanded the preservation and worship,—reverence rather than worship in the modern English use of the words,—of the icons as a security for the remembrance of the Manhood of the Lord. The worship was not λατρεία, which can be paid to God alone, but προσκύνησις σχετική. Christ, said S. Theodore, was in danger of losing the quality of being man if not seen and worshipped in an image.

The long dispute ended, as we have said, after the accession of the Empress Irene, who, unworthy though she was to have part in any great religious movement, yet had always been attached to the traditional opinions of the Greek people. The monks of Constantinople had exercised a steady influence during all the years of disturbance: and they were to triumph. The Empress Irene replaced the patriarch Paul in 783 by her own secretary Tarasius, and it was determined at once to reverse the decrees that

The
Seventh
General
Council,
787.

had been passed at Constantinople in 754. In 787 for the second time a council met at Nicæa, across the Sea of Marmora, which became recognised as the Seventh General Council. To it came representatives of East and West, and the decision which was arrived at was practically that of the whole Church.

The persecution of the orthodox was renewed for a time under Leo V. (813–20), and it is said that more perished in his time than in that of Constantine V. Theophilus (829–42) was almost equally hostile. It was not till his widow Theodora assumed the reins of power in 842 as regent for her son that the final triumph of orthodoxy was assured; and this was followed by the five years' patriarchate of S. Metho-dius, a man of peace and of wisdom.

To some the action of the emperors in attacking image worship has seemed a serious attempt at social reform, an endeavour to raise the standard of popular worship, and through that to affect the people them-selves intellectually, morally, and spiritually. But history has spoken conclusively of the violence with which the attempt was made, and theology has deci-sively pronounced against its dogmatic assertions.

The long controversy is important in the history of the Church because it so clearly expresses the character of the Eastern Church, so decisively demonstrates its intense devotion to the past, and so expressively illustrates the close attachment, the abiding influence, of the people and the monks, as the dominant factor in the development of theology and religious life.

CHAPTER XV

LEARNING AND MONASTICISM

SOMETHING has been said in earlier chapters of the relation of several great Churchmen towards education, towards the ancient classics, and towards the studies of their own times. Something has been said, too, in the last chapter, of Greek monastic life. The period which begins with the eighth century deserves a longer mention, inadequate though it be; for there was over a great part of Europe in the days of Charles the Great a veritable literary renaissance which broke upon the long period which men have called the dark ages with a ray of light.

Charles the Great had all the interests of a scholar. He knew Latin well and Greek passably. He delighted to listen to the deeds of the past, or to theological treatises, when he dined, after the fashion of monks. His interest in learning centred in his interest in the teaching and services of the Church. Most reverently, we are told by his biographer, and with the utmost piety did he cultivate the Christian religion with which he had been imbued from his infancy. He was a constant church-goer, a regular worshipper at the mass. Near to his religious interest was his interest in education. A famous letter of his to the abbats of monasteries

Learning at the court of Charles the Great.

throughout the Empire, written in 787, is a salient example of the close connection between learning and monasticism in his day. He urged that "letters" should be studied, students selected and taught, that all the clergy should teach children freely, and that every monastery and cathedral church should have a theological school. " Although right doing is better than right speaking," he wrote, " yet must the know-ledge of what is right go before the doing of it."

What he tried to do throughout his empire was a reflection of what he did in his own court. He delighted to surround himself at Aachen with learned men. Most notable among them were Paul the Deacon, the historian of the Lombards, and Alcuin the Northumbrian whom he had met in Italy and whom he made prominent among his counsellors.

Charles, says Einhard, spent much time and labour in learning from Alcuin, and that not only in religion, but "in rhetoric and dialectic and especially astronomy"; and he " carefully reformed the manner of reading and singing; for he was thoroughly instructed in both, though he never read publicly himself, nor sang except in a low voice, and with the rest of the congregation."

Alcuin connects the learning of England with the revival on the Continent. He had been trained in the school at York by Archbishop Egbert, who was himself a pupil of Bede. He had studied the ancient classics in Greek as well as Latin and knew at least a little of Hebrew. The library at York is known to have contained books in all those languages, and Aristotle was among them. Vergil, he said, when he was a boy he cared more for than the vigils of the Church and the chanting of the

Alcuin of Northum-bria.

psalms. About 782 he took charge of the schools
which Charles had founded at his court, and he became
a very close friend and trusted adviser of the emperor
himself. With him (but for a short return to England)
he lived till in 796 he had leave to retire to Tours,
where he was abbat of the great monastery of
S. Martin, and where he died in 804. He was a great
teacher; a writer of books of education and books of
Church practice, of lives of the saints, of hymns,
epigrams, prayers, controversial tracts; a compiler of
summaries of patristic teaching; a leader in the reform
of monastic houses. Among the many notable points
in his career, as illustrating the life of learned churchmen of his age, are two especially to be observed. The
first is his "humanism." He was a scholar of an ancient
type; and the society in which he lived delighted to
believe itself classical as well as Christian. In a contemporary description of the life at Charles's court
Alcuin is called "Flaccus" and is described as "the
glory of our bards, mighty to shout forth his songs,
keeping time with his lyric foot, moreover a powerful
sophist, able to prove pious doctrines out of Holy
Scripture, and in genial jest to propose or solve puzzles
of arithmetic." As a theologian he was most famous
for his books against Felix of Urgel and Elipandus of
Toledo, on the subject of the Adoptianist heresy (see
above, ch. vi), and there is no doubt that his was an
important influence in the Council of Frankfort which
condemned them. The second is his attitude towards
the monastic life. He admired the monastic life, but
he had not been trained as a strict Benedictine, indeed
he was probably no more than a secular in deacon's
orders. He held abbeys as their superior, just as many

laymen did; but he never seems to have been inclined to take upon him any strict rule. His example shows how natural was the next step in monastic history which is associated with the abbey of Cluny.

In Alcuin England was linked to the wider world of Christendom. This has been summarily expressed by a great English historian thus: "The The schools of Northumbria had gathered in the schools of harvest of Irish learning, of the Franco- Europe. Gallican schools still subsisting and preserving a remnant of classical character in the sixth century, and of Rome, itself now barbarised. Bede had received instruction from the disciples of Chad and Cuthbert in the Irish studies of the Scriptures, from Wilfrid and Acca in the French and Roman learning, and from Benedict Biscop and Albinus in the combined and organised discipline of Theodore. By his influence with Egbert, the school of York was founded, and in it was centred nearly all the wisdom of the West, and its great pupil was Alcuin. Whilst learning had been growing in Northumbria, it had been declining on the Continent; in the latter days of Alcuin, the decline of English learning began in consequence of the internal dissensions of the kings, and the early ravages of the Northmen. Just at the same time the Continent was gaining peace and organisation under Charles. Alcuin carried the learning which would have perished in England into France and Germany, where it was maintained whilst England relapsed into the state of ignorance from which it was delivered by Alfred. Alcuin was rather a man of learning and action than of genius and contemplation like Bede, but his power of organisation and of teaching was great, and his services to religion and literature in Europe, based indeed on the foundation of Bede, were more widely extended and in themselves inestimable." [1]

Side by side with the career of Alcuin, of which much is known, may be placed that of another scholar who was at least equally influential, but of whose life little is known. John the Scot, whose thought exercised a profound influence on the ages after his death, was one of the Irish scholars whom the famous schools of that island produced as late as the ninth century. He became attached to the court of Charles the Bald, as Alcuin had been to that of Charles the Great. He became like Alcuin a prominent defender of the faith, being invited by Hincmar, Archbishop of Rheims, to answer the monk Gottschalk's exaggerated doctrine of predestination, which went much farther than S. Augustine, and might be described as Calvinist before Calvin ; but his arguments were also considered unsound, and his opinions were condemned in later synods. The argument that, evil being the negation of good, God could not know it, for with Him to know is to cause, was certainly weak if not formally heretical, and his subtleties seemed to the theologians of his time to be merely ineptitudes. He was also, it is at least probable, engaged in the controversy on the doctrine of the Holy Eucharist which began about this time, originating in the treatise of Paschasius Radbertus, *de Sacramento Corporis et Sanguinis Christi.* In 1050 a treatise bearing John the Scot's name was condemned; but it seems that this was really written by Ratramnus of Corbie. The view of Radbert was that which was after-

John Scotus.

[1] Bp. Stubbs in *Dict. of Christian Biography*, vol. i. p. 74.

wards formalised into Transubstantiation. The view
attributed to John was a clear denial of any material-
ising doctrine of the Sacrament. Later writers say that
John returned to England, taught in the abbey school
at Malmesbury, the famous school originated by Irish
monks and illustrated by the fame of S. Aldhelm, and
there died. His chief work was the *de Divisione
Naturae*, in which he seems to anticipate much later
philosophic argument (notably that of S. Anselm and
Descartes as to the existence of God) and to have
been the precursor if not the founder of Nominalism.

With John the Scot it is clear that both the old
literature and philosophy survived and were fruitful
and that new interests, which would carry theology
into further developments, were arising. A revival of
learning was naturally the growth of the monastic
system; but that system was itself far from secure at
the time of which we speak.

The Benedictine rule did not win its way over
Europe without some checks; nor was it always able
to retain its hold in an age of general dis-   The
order. Much depended upon the abbat in   Benedic-
each particular house. In Gaul, the rule of   tine rule.
S. Columban had made him absolute. But such a
submission was never accepted in central and southern
Gaul. From the end of the sixth century it is clear
that monasticism was beginning to slacken its devotion. The history of the monastery of S. Radegund as
given by Gregory of Tours shows this; so does the letter
of Gregory the Great to Brunichild. Nor did the milder
rule of S. Benedict long remain unaltered in practice.

A new revival is connected with the names of Odo
and Cluny.

Saint Odo emerges from an age in which the most striking feature was the reassertion of the imperial power and the imperial idea. The ninth century, as it began, witnessed a remarkable revival, the revival of a decayed and dormant institution—the Roman Empire —in whose ashes there had yet survived the fire which had inspired the rulers of the world in the past. The great idea of imperialism was reborn in the person of a man of extraordinary physical and mental power, a sovereign who, while he had not a little of the weaknesses of his age, had also in a remarkable degree centred in himself its highest philosophic aspirations. The early ninth century is dominated by the figure of Charles the Great. The result was inevitable. Lay power, lay over-lordship or supremacy, extends everywhere, intrudes into the recesses of monastic life, and dictates even in things purely spiritual. And as the new tide of barbarian invasion, Saracen or Norman, sweeps on in Spain or Gaul, the Church, for very physical needs, seeks refuge under the protection of lay barons, princes, and kings. Feudalism is rising. The monastic houses fall often under the arrogant rule of lay abbats. And the popes, not rarely a prey themselves to the vices of the age, sink into impotence and become enmeshed in worldly, often shameful, intrigue and disorder. The canons of Church councils show that it was below as it was above. Secularity was general, vice was far from rare.

The Divine spirit and the past history of Christianity made it certain that a revival of life must come. The dry bones would feel the breath and would live

The decay of monasticism in the ninth century.

again. On the borders of the lands of Maine and
Anjou was born in 879, of a line of feudal barons,
Odo, the regenerator of monasticism, the
ultimate reviver of the papacy, the spiritual **S. Odo.**
progenitor of Hildebrand himself. Promised to God
at his birth, he was long held back by his father for
knighthood and the life of a warrior such as he himself had led; a grievous sickness gave him, on his
recovery, to the monastic life. The disciple alike of
S. Martin and S. Benedict, he took inspiration from
them to revive the strict monastic rule. From a
canon he became a monk, after a noviciate at Baume,
the foundation of Columban in the wild and beautiful
valley between the Seille and the Dard, in the diocese
of Besançon. For a time he tasted the life of the
anchorite and the cœnobite. Then he passed to the
abbey of Cluny, founded in 910 by William of
Aquitaine in the mountains above the valley of the
Grosne, and ruled till 927 by Berno, who came himself from Baume. On his death Odo became abbat;
and to him the great development of the revival of
strict monasticism is due.

Cluny became the type of the exempted abbeys,
and the highest representative of the monastic
privileges. It embodied in itself the best
expression of the resistance to feudalism; **Cluny.**
it became the most powerful support of the papacy
and of the much-needed movement for the reform of
the Church. The first necessity of the new monasticism was an absolute independence of the lay
power. Thus the founder attached it from the first
to the Roman Church, and gave up all his own rights
of property. Its situation, in the heart of Burgundy,

removed it from the power of the king. Charles the Simple permitted its foundation, Louis d'Outremer confirmed its privileges. When Urban II., a militant Cluniac, became pope the interests of Cluny and Rome were more than ever identified. The monks elected their abbat without exterior interference. To prevent this becoming an abuse, the first abbats always proposed their coadjutors as their successors. Thus it was with Berno (910–27), Odo (927–48), Maieul (948-94), Odilo (990-1049). After that there arose the custom of appointing the grand prior as successor — as in the case of S. Hugh (1049–1109). From the confirmation of its foundation in 931 by John XI. Cluny received the greatest favours at the hands of the papacy, its abbats being created arch-abbots with episcopal insignia; and it was made entirely independent of the bishops.

Cluny soon attracted attention, wealth, and followers. Corrupt old communities or new foundations sought the guidance or protection of its abbats. **The rule of Cluny.** When each monastery was independent and isolated it was impossible to reform a lax community, or for it to defend itself from feudal violence and the hostility of the secular clergy. Odo, the saint who saw these evils, therefore started what soon became the Congregation of Cluny. The daughter-houses were regarded not as independent, but as parts of Cluny. There was only one abbat, the arch-abbat of Cluny, who was the head of all. Necessary local control was exercised by the prior, responsible to and nominated by the abbat. Some houses resisted annexation to Cluny, such as S. Martial at Limoges, which kept up the contest from 1063 to 1240. Contact between the abbey and its dependencies was preserved by visitation of the abbat; and the dependent houses sent representatives to periodical chapters, which met at Cluny under the abbat. In the eleventh century these were merely consultative, but in the thirteenth they had become political, administrative, and judicial, even subjecting the abbat to their control. The rule of S. Benedict was followed in the abbey and its dependencies. The monks did some manual labour, but devoted themselves chiefly to religious exercises, to teaching the young, to hospitality and almsgiving.

But the Cluniacs, protected by the papacy, and enriched by the offerings of the faithful all over Europe, taught an extreme doctrine as to the power of the Holy See. Their ideal was the absolute separation of Church from State, the reorganisation of the Church under a general discipline such as could be exercised only by the pope. He, in their ideal, was to stand towards the whole world as the Cluniac abbat stood towards each Cluniac priory, the one ultimate source of jurisdiction, the Universal Bishop, appointing and degrading the diocesan bishops as the abbat made and unmade the priors.

How much of all this did the great Odo plan ? Not very much. But it was his work to revive the discipline, the holiness, the self-sacrifice, which, through the reformed monasteries, should touch the whole Church.

And thus monasticism at the beginning of the eleventh century was a wholly new force in the life of Christendom. It was destined to reform the papacy itself.

CHAPTER XVI

SACRAMENTS AND LITURGIES

IN the centuries with which we deal the importance of Baptism cannot be overrated. It was everywhere, in all the missions of the Church, regarded as the critical point of the individual life and the indispensable means of entrance to the **Baptism.** Christian Church. When the children of Sebert the king of the East Saxons wished to have all the privileges of Christians, which their father had had, and "a share in the white bread" though they were still heathen, Mellitus the bishop answered, "If you will be washed in that font of salvation in which your father was washed, then you may also partake of the holy bread of which he used to partake: but if you despise the laver of life you cannot possibly receive the bread of life"; and he was driven from the kingdom because he would not yield an inch. The tale however shows also that there were still on the fringe of Christianity persons who were not baptized, not catechumens, yet still interested in the religion and to some extent anxious to be sharers in its life. Throughout the early history of Gaulish Christianity the same is to be observed, and it is doubtless the reason why a number of semi-pagan customs still survived among those who were nominally Christians, as well as those who still stood outside the Church. Baptism in the case of many was a critical point in the history of a tribe or nation. The baptism of Chlodowech was the greatest historical event in the history of the Franks: it was of critical importance that the Franks, with him, accepted orthodox Christianity, that he, robed in the white vesture which West and East alike considered meet, and which was sometimes worn for the octave after baptism, confessed his faith in the Blessed Trinity, was baptized in the name of Father, Son and Holy Ghost, and was anointed with the holy chrism and signed with the sign of the cross.   Baptism not only admitted into the Christian Church, but was invested with the associations of the human family, and thus had transferred to it some of the conditions in which students of anthropology find such interesting survivals of primitive ideas.   The conception of spiritual relationship was endowed with the results which belonged to natural kinship.   The sponsors became spiritual parents.   The code of Justinian forbade the marriage of a godchild and godparent, because "nothing can so much call out fatherly affection and the just prohibition of marriage as a bond of this kind, by means of which, through the action of God, their souls are united to one another." This led to the growth of as elaborate a scheme of spiritual relationships as that which already hedged round among many tribes the eligibility for marriage among persons even remotely akin to one another. In the East, as in the West, baptism was most frequently conferred at the time of the great Christian festivals, Christmas (as in the case of Chlodowech), Epiphany, and especially Easter; and Easter Eve became, later

N

on, especially consecrated to the sacred rite. In the East baptism was often postponed till the infant was two years old; and everywhere there was for long a tendency even among Christian parents to hold back children from the laver of regeneration for fear of the consequences of post-baptismal sin. It was thus that a name was often given, and a child received into the Church, some weeks or even months before the baptism took place. The Greek Syntagma of the seventh century contains interesting information as to the baptism of heretics. It is ordered that Sabellians, Montanists, Manichæans, Valentianists and such like shall be baptized just as pagans are, after instruction and examination in the faith, and, after insufflation, by triple immersion.

Throughout these centuries baptism was not separated from Confirmation, except in the case of some converts from heresy. The two rites were regarded as parts of the same sacrament, or at least the former was not considered complete without the latter. The sacramental life of the individual in fact was to begin with his entrance into the Church and never to be intermitted. Even infants were present throughout the celebration of the sacred mysteries and partook of the Communion, a custom which was only abandoned in the West because of the difficulty of frequent giving of Confirmation and the consequent delay of that rite till later years.

Baptism and Confirmation was the gate by which the Christian was admitted to the Sacrament of the Lord's Body and Blood. The celebration of that Sacrament was the chief act of the Church's worship every Sunday and holy day, and in

Confirmation.

The Holy Communion.

Spain, Africa, Antioch, daily, in Rome every day except Friday and Saturday, in Alexandria except on
Thursday and Friday: indeed by the end of the sixth
century it seems probable that in most parts of the
Church a daily celebration was usual. From the
seventh century the mass of the presanctified, when the
priest communicated from elements previously consecrated, is found in use on certain days, and in the East
throughout except on Saturdays and Sundays. It
seems clear that at least up to the sixth century it was
usual for all who were confirmed to com-   Frequent
municate whenever they were present,   Com-
unless they were under penance; but the   munion.
custom of noncommunicating attendance was growing
up. In the East a spiritual writer said, "it is not
rare or frequent communion which matters, but to
make a good communion with a prepared conscience ";
while in the West Bede's letter to Archbishop Egbert
of York supplies an excellent illustration of
custom. The people are to be told, he ad-   Bede.
vises, " how salutary it is for all classes of Christians to
participate daily in the body and blood of our Lord, as
you know well is done by Christ's Church throughout
Italy,'Gaul, Africa, Greece, and all the countries of the
East. Now, this kind of religion and heavenly devotion, through the neglect of our teachers, has been so
long discontinued among almost all the laity of our
province, that those who seem to be most religious
among them communicate in the holy mysteries only
on the Day of our Lord's birth, the Epiphany, and
Easter, whilst there are innumerable boys and girls, of
innocent and chaste life, as well as young men and
women, old men and old women, who without any scruple

or debate are able to communicate in the holy mysteries on every Lord's Day, nay, on all the birthdays of the holy Apostles and martyrs, as you have yourself seen done in the holy Roman and Apostolic Church." It would seem from this that frequent communion was inculcated by the first missionaries to England in the sixth century. Bede tells also how in his day two Anglian priests went on a mission to the heathen Saxons, and, while waiting for the decision of the "satrap," "devoted themselves to prayer and psalm-singing, and daily offered to God the sacrifice of the Saving Victim, having with them sacred vessels and a hallowed table to serve as an altar."

The Sacrament was received in both kinds and fasting, and the priest was forbidden to celebrate after **Fasting** taking any food; some exception to this **Commu-** rule may be inferred from a canon of the **nion.** Second Council of Mâcon in 585 enforcing it, and the ecclesiastical historian Socrates (whose History extends from 306 to 439) states that some in Egypt did not receive "as the custom is among Christians," but after a meal. The presence of the Lord in the Eucharist was recognised and adored. S. Anastasius of Sinai, probably of the sixth century, writes: "After **The** the bloodless sacrifice has been consecrated, **doctrine** the priest lifts up the bread of life, and **of the** shows it to all." The Eucharist is con- **Sacrifice.** tinually spoken of as the holy Sacrifice, the offering of the Saving Victim, the Celestial Oblation; and it was offered, as the writings of Gregory the Great show, in special intercession for the dead as well as the living. From the beginning of the fifth century it seems to have been, at least occasionally, reserved in church as well as sent to the sick in their own houses.

During the fifth and sixth centuries it would seem that the Roman mass, the rite which has slowly superseded the local forms of service in most parts of Europe, was undergoing the modifications which brought it to the stereo- typed form it now has. The severe, terse, practical nature of the liturgy, in words, ritual, ceremonial, which is so characteristic of the Roman nature, was being altered by the admixture of other elements. This was especially the case, it is said, in France and Germany, during the ninth century. Earlier changes had been made by Gregory the Great, partly from Eastern sources. At the middle of the fifth century the rite, in words and action alike, was a simple one. The choir sang an in- troit, the priest a collect, epistle and gospel were read, and a psalm was sung: the gifts were offered, the prayer or "preface" of the day was followed by the *Sanctus*, as in the East, and then came the Canon or actual Consecration. After this was the Lord's Prayer, communion of priests, clergy and people, a psalm and a collect and the end. The ceremonial was equally simple, and was connected almost exclu- sively with the entrance of the celebrant and his ministers, at which incense was used, and with the reading of the gospel, where also lights and incense were prominent. All else was simple and of dignified reticence. "Mystery never flourished in the clear Roman atmosphere, and symbolism was no product of the Roman religious mind. Christian symbolism is not of pure Roman birth, not a native product of the

Roman spirit."[1] This reticent character is most clearly found in the Gregorian missal, which has been believed to represent the period of Gregory the Great. More probably the assertion of John the Deacon that Gregory revised the Gelasian Sacramentary is an error, and what is called the Gregorian Sacramentary is simply the book which was sent by Pope Hadrian I. to Charles I. between 784 and 791.   But that S. Gregory did make certain alterations is certain. They were three in the Liturgy, two in the ceremonial of the mass. The Alleluia was ordered to be more frequently chanted than before; and we find it used outside the Easter season almost immediately after this by S. Augustine in England. He added words to the "Hanc igitur" in the Canon of the mass, praying for peace and inclusion in the number of the elect. He inserted the Lord's Prayer immediately after the Canon. He also forbade the deacons to sing any of the mass except the gospel and the subdeacons to wear chasubles at the altar.

It is thought that the great change, which made the Roman mass into the elaborate rite it became, is due to the influence, at the end of the eighth century, of Charles the Great, who with the determination of a ruler and the interest of a liturgiologist made one rite to be observed throughout his dominions, but enriched the Gregorian book with details and ceremonies derived from uses already common in France. The study of liturgies became common in the ninth century, and in Gaul additions were made to the book sent by Pope Hadrian

The eighth century.

---

[1] Edmund Bishop, "The Genesis of the Roman Rite," in *Essays on Ceremonial*, 1904.

to Charles the Great, which were finally accepted throughout the greater part of Italy, the Ambrosian rite in the province of Milan remaining different throughout the changes.

It is natural that English readers should desire to know more particularly of the first English Christian worship. How did the Church's worship first begin in our own land?

No doubt the Christians who received conversion during the Roman occupation of Britain, and those of Ireland who were won by the preaching of S. Patrick, worshipped according to the same rite as the churches of Spain or the churches of Gaul, following that use which survived in Spain generally till the eleventh century and in Gaul till the ninth. Gildas, who wrote during the stress of the conquest of the Christian Brythons by the heathen English, mentions one custom which undoubtedly was Gallican, and which is preserved in the Gelasian Sacramentary and the *Missale Francorum*, the one a Roman collection which contains Gallican uses, the other a Gallican rite. It is that of anointing the hands of priests, and perhaps deacons, in ordination, and the custom was kept up after the conversion of the English, at least in some parts of England in the tenth and eleventh centuries. But the influence of the British Church was slight. It is of more interest to us to know what was the first worship offered in this land by those who were to convert our own forefathers.

The rites of the Western isles.

Bede tells us how first Augustine prayed when he came before the heathen king of Kent. Some days after their landing Æthelbert received the monks from

Rome. They had tarried, it seems probable, under the
S. Augustine in Kent. walls of the old Roman fortress of Richborough. They had waited, in prayer and patience, for the beginning of their Mission.
It was on prayer that they still depended when they were summoned before the king. On a ridge of rocks overlooking the sea sat Æthelbert and his gesiths, and watched the band of some forty men draw near. Slowly they came, and the strange sound of the Church's music was wafted to the ears of the heathen company as they drew near. Before them was borne a tall silver cross, and a banner which displayed the pictured image of the Saviour Lord,

> The Cross preceding Him who floats in air,
> The pictured Saviour.

S. Gregory, the great pope who had sent the mission, who had himself long dwelt at the court of the emperors in Constantinople, had learnt the value of *icons*, of sacred pictures, as texts for an appeal, or as stimulants to devotion. Those who cannot read, he said, should be taught by pictures, but pictures are valuable only because they point to Him whom we adore as incarnate, crucified, sitting at the right hand of God. As they came, they sang, and Bede says : " they sang litanies, entreating the Lord for their own salvation and that of those for whom and to whom they came." The litany ended when they came to the king, and then Augustine preached the word. He declared, says an old English writer of later days, " how the merciful Saviour with His own sufferings redeemed their guilty world, and opened an entrance into the kingdom of heaven to all faithful men."

The king bade them deliver their message, and they

sat—for it was no formal sermon, but rather, as we should say, a meditation on the things of God—and "preached the word of life to him and all his gesiths who were present." Bede tells us the answer of the grave thoughtful Æthelbert—"They are certainly beautiful words and promises that you bring; but because they are new and unproved, I cannot give my assent to them and give up those things which I with all the English race have so long observed. But since you are strangers and have come a long way, so that—as I think I can see clearly—you might impart to us that which you believe to be true and most good, I do not wish you any harm, but rather will treat you kindly and see that you have all you need, and we will not hinder you from bringing over to the faith of your own religion all of our people that you can win." And so he gave them lodging in his own city, the metropolis, as Bede, as it were by prophecy, calls it, of Canterbury. Towards Canterbury they went, still with litany and procession, and thus, Bede tells us, it is said they sang—still carrying the holy cross and the picture of the great King, our Lord Jesus Christ.—

The litanies.

"We beseech Thee, O Lord, according to all Thy mercy, that Thy wrath and Thine anger may be turned away from this city, and from Thy holy house; for we have sinned. Alleluia."

A tradition that lasted down to Bede's own day thus handed down their words. There is great interest in this picture of Christian worship in the heathen land, our own, that was to be won for Christ. It illustrates the worship of the land the missionaries came from, as well as serves as a pattern for the worship which the

English, under Augustine's guidance, should follow.
What was this litany? Litanies at Rome were regu-
lated by S. Gregory himself, and he was very likely
only revising and setting in order a form of service
already well known. But this very litany S. Augustine and his companions had most likely heard during
their passage through Gaul. There the Rogation
litanies had been over a hundred years in use; and
these words form part of a Rogation litany used long
after in Vienne, through which doubtless Augustine
travelled. Thus the missionaries were using a part of
the Gallican service-books, and not of the Roman; and
the Rogation procession, which lasted so long in
England, which still lingers in some places in the form
of "beating the bounds," and which in late years has
been here and there revived among us, comes to us
with Augustine from Gaul, and not from Rome, where
it was not yet in use. "Alleluia!" too, a strange
ending to a penitential litany in modern ears, was the
close of Gallican litanies at Rogationtide, as later in
Christian England itself, and its use outside the Easter
season was especially authorised by Gregory the Great.
And if Augustine's own first public prayers were Gallican, so most probably was the use of the chapel of the
Kentish Queen Bercta, who was daughter of the West
Frankish king, and who had with her a Frankish
bishop, Liudhard. But his own use would be the
Roman, just as his own manner of chanting, long preserved at Canterbury, was after the manner of the
Romans. And thus, with the strong sense of unity
natural to a man trained in the school of the great
Gregory, Augustine was startled at the contrast of
customs when it came to him in practical guise. Why,

the faith being one, are there the different customs of
different churches, and one manner of masses in the
holy Roman church, another in that of the Gauls ? So
he asked the great teacher who had sent him. A wise
answer came from the wise pope, disclaiming all pecu-
liar authority or special sanctity for the use of Rome.
" Things are not to be loved for the sake of places, but
places for the sake of things." " Select, then," he
advises, " from many churches, whatever you have
found in Gaul, or in Rome, or in any other church,
that is good; make a rite for the new church of the
English, such as you think pious and best."

All this, when Augustine's position is remembered,
will be seen to show how far Rome then was from
arrogating to herself any strange supremacy
such as later days have brought. The first
primate of the English was allowed freedom
to make an English rite. But, on the other hand, we
have no evidence that he did so. He preferred, we
have every reason to believe, the Roman rite, with
only here and there a few changes or additions. The
Council of Clovesho, presided over by Cuthbert, Archbishop of Canterbury, in 747, followed in his steps,
taking in regard to rites " the model which we have in
writing from the Roman Church." But none the less
later English service-books show very considerable
Gallican influence. Celtic missionaries, and the connection four centuries later with Gaul and Burgundy,
left traces in the way in which the service was per-
formed; and England, up to the Reformation, like all
other countries indeed, had some distinct customs of
its own. Throughout the long history of conversion
which spreads over the whole island, it is noteworthy

*English
uses.*

that preaching and the singing of litanies, as at the first coming of Augustine, are conspicuous in the methods of the saints who won England to Christ.

What then was the service of the Holy Communion, as S. Augustine celebrated it, and our English fore-fathers first came to know it? If, as we suppose, it was the Roman, it would proceed thus. First an anti-phon, which came to be called an introit, or psalm of entrance, with a verse having special reference to the lesson of the day or season, was sung, as the priest, wearing a long white surplice or alb and a chasuble (the robe worn alike by lay and by clerical officials), entered with two deacons, wearing probably similar garments. In the Gallican rite, as in the eastern, there followed the singing of the " Trisagion " : and in both Gallican and Roman the " Kyrie Eleeson," as in our own office to-day, though we now add to it a special prayer for grace to keep the Commandments. Then in the Roman rite was sung the " Gloria in Excelsis," while in the Gallican the " Benedictus " took its place. This was introductory. Now came the collect, the prayer when all the people were gathered together. Then the Lesson from the Old Testament, the Epistle, and the Gospel. Between the Old Testament Lesson and the Epistle was sung the " Gradual," a psalm sung from the steps of the ambo or pulpit, but gradually the use of Rome was followed all over Europe, and the Old Testament reading was omitted altogether. After the Epistle was sung " Alleluia " or the psalm called the Tract. Then the Gospel was sung, introduced with special solemnity. The deacon mounted the pulpit, seven candles being carried before him, and the choir

The Eucharist in the sixth century.

chanting "Glory be to Thee, O Lord." After the deacon had read the Gospel, a sermon was generally preached, but the Creed was at this time not said. A short common prayer followed (in the Gallican rite a litany), and then the mass of the catechumens was over, and those who were unbaptized or unworthy to remain at that time for the consecration departed from the church, a custom which has survived in England under changed conditions.

Then, when the faithful only remained, the offertory was sung, and the bread and wine and water were offered (the ceremonial was different and much longer in the Gallican rite, and included the kiss of peace). S. Augustine, if he followed the Roman use, would offer the bread and wine himself, with the laity assisting: the Gallican use was to prepare the elements before-hand, and now bring them into church in procession. The priest then washed his hands and said privately a collect, while in the Gallican rite he read from the dip-tychs, or tablets of the church, the names of those de-parted who were to be especially commemorated.

Then followed the prayer called the Preface, and the singing of " Holy, Holy, Holy." After this, in the Gallican rite, came a special prayer, and then, as still in the Mozarabic, followed the recital of our Lord's institution of the Sacrament, as in the English Prayer-book now ; but the Roman rite had also prayers for the Church, for the living and dead, and both united in the prayer (called *paraklesis*) that the elements might receive consecration from God, which was the consecra-tion itself until much later. Then the dead and living were again prayed for, and the fruits of the earth were dedicated by prayer.

The Lord's Prayer, by the order of S. Gregory himself, concluded this part of the service, which came to be known as the Canon, the invariable part of the Mass. In the Roman rite the kiss of peace followed, the faithful kissing each other according to the ancient custom. Then the priest broke the bread, and said the Lord's Prayer alone till the last clause. Then he placed a piece of the bread in the cup, and received the Sacrament himself, afterwards giving it in one kind to the clergy and laity, while the deacon followed with the chalice. Before the Communion it was a custom taken from Gaul, which lasted in England up to the Reformation, that the Bishop, if present, should bless the people. A hymn was sung during the communion of the people; the ancient "Draw nigh and take the Body of the Lord" remains still to us from a Celtic source for use at this time. The service ended with a "Let us pray" and collect after Communion, closely followed by the second of the alternative post-communion prayers now in our English office. Immediately after this prayer the deacon said "Ite, missa est" ("Go: it is the dismissal").

In the English services to-day, while much is changed, and the language is our own, we can still trace very much that has been used continuously since the day when S. Augustine first said the whole office of the Church on British soil.

Much more might be said; but this may suffice to illustrate the interest and importance which belong to sacraments and liturgical rites in the ages of which we speak.

CHAPTER XVII

THE END OF THE DARK AGE

AS we draw to the close of the long period which, through the conversion of the barbarian races and the growth of a central power in the Church at Rome, so profoundly influenced the future of the world, we are met by some **The end of the age.** outstanding facts which mark an epoch of crisis and of reformation. They are—the widening breach in matters religious, as earlier in matters political, between East and West; the influences which served to strengthen the theory of the papal monarchy even at the time of its greatest practical weakness; and the strength of the Empire under the Saxon Ottos as a power to unite Western Europe and to reform the Western Church.

Nicolas, who was elected in 858, was a great pope. He asserted the moral force of Christianity in a way in which his predecessors very frequently followed him, by vindicating the indissolubility of the marriage tie. Chlo- **The papacy of Nicolas I., 858-67.** thochar, King of Lotharingia, separated from his wife Theudberga, bringing against her foul charges, which a council of clergy at Aachen accepted. Nicolas intervened: again and again he endeavoured to control the Frankish clergy and rescind the divorce; but it was only in 863 by a council at Rome, where the archbishops of Cologne and Trier were present, that he was able to proceed to extremities. He excommunicated those two prelates, and deposed them with all those who had assisted them: he warned Hincmar of Rheims of what he had done. The emperor Louis, Chlothochar's brother, marched on Rome and captured the city; but there, through illness it appears, he completely submitted to the pope. Nicolas enforced his decision on the Frankish king, the Frankish bishops, on Hincmar, the great archbishop of Rheims himself. In a letter he developed the theory that the Empire owed its confirmation to the authority of the Apostolic See, and that the sword was conferred on the emperor by the pope, the vicar of S. Peter. Truly it was said of this pope by one who wrote a century after his death, "Since the days of Gregory to our own sat no prelate on the throne of S. Peter to be compared to Nicolas. He tamed king and tyrants and ruled the world like a monarch: to holy bishops he was mild and gentle: to the wicked and unconverted a terror; so that truly may we say that in him arose a new Elijah."

Of equal though different importance was the action of the papacy in regard to the East. What is known as the Photian schism is the divergence between the churches of Constantinople and Rome, which became critical during the pontificate of Nicolas I.

Photius, a man of great learning and experience, a scholar and theologian of the familiar Greek type,
The Photian schism. was elected Patriarch of Constantinople on Christmas Day, 857. At the time when Michael III. determined on his appointment he was not even ordained: in six days he

received the different orders and was made patriarch. But his election was uncanonical. Ignatius the
patriarch, who was still living, was deposed because
of his censures of the emperor's evil life. Photius
announced his election to Pope Nicolas, but Ignatius
refused to surrender his rights; both parties excommunicated each other; and the emperor mocked at
both. But he also asked the pope to send legates to
a council which should restore order to the Church.
The Council met in 861. It confirmed Photius in his
office, and the papal legates assented. Nicolas refused
to accept the decision and took upon him to annul it, to
depose Photius, to declare the orders conferred by him
invalid, and to announce his decision to the other
patriarchs and to the metropolitans and bishops who
owed obedience to Constantinople. Neither the
emperor nor Photius would submit; and in 867
Photius issued, in a council at Constantinople, an
encyclical letter, in which he repudiated the papal
claim of jurisdiction (which was complicated by assertions of supremacy over the Bulgarian Church), and
denounced a number of tenets held by Westerns,
and most notably the addition of the word
Filioque to the Nicene Creed, as asserting
the procession of the Holy Spirit from the
Father and the Son. He ended by excom-
municating the pope.

The Filioque contro-versy.

In the year 867 Nicolas died, Michael was deposed,
Photius followed him into retirement, Basil the Macedonian ascended the throne, and Ignatius was restored
to the patriarchate. A council was held in 869 at
which papal legates attended, which approved these
acts, and which is counted by the Roman Church as

o

the Eighth Œcumenical Council. This Council confirmed the Church's decision as to image-worship. Ignatius held his throne till his death in 877, when Photius was reinstated. His return was signalised by a new agreement with Rome, in which Pope John VIII. repudiated the insertion of the *Filioque*, and declared that it was inserted by men whose daring was due to madness, and who were transgressors against the Divine Word. Another council at Constantinople (879–80) confirmed the reinstatement, declared Photius to be lawful patriarch, and anathematised the Council of 869. This is reckoned by the Greeks as the Eighth Œcumenical Council. Then the schism was for the time healed. It made no difference that a new emperor, Leo VI., the Wise, deposed Photius again and appointed his own brother. The union remained formally throughout the tenth century. But though the eleventh century opened with a nominal agreement, it was not destined to endure. The points of severance must be dealt with in a later volume. It may here suffice to say that the position of the Greeks was rigidly conservative, of the popes aggressively authoritative.

End of the schism.

It was an age of growing papal claims; and the claims had now found a new basis.

The promises, true and legendary, of Pippin, and the spurious donation of Constantine, had still further extension in the False Decretals. These were first used by Nicolas I., who was pope from 858 to 867. During his pontificate the collection of Church laws, with the canons of the Œcumenical Councils, the letters of the most important bishops and the like, with the ecclesiastical laws of the

The forged decretals.

emperors, which were practically becoming a *corpus juris canonici*, received a notable addition. The genuine decretals of the popes begin with Siricius (384–98); but there now (between 840 and 860) appeared fifty-nine more, professing to date from the second and third centuries, and also thirty-nine became interpolated among the genuine documents, which ranged from 386 to 731. These were put forth by a skilful forger as the collection of Isidore of Seville, and they were incorporated in the authentic collection made by him. A most remarkable series of documents was this, in every point supporting the claims now put forth by the Roman See to political as well as ecclesiastical supremacy, deciding questions of discipline and right such as were then vexed, and supplying a veritable armoury for the advocates of papal claims to rule everywhere, over all persons, and in all causes. The forged decretals, now known as the pseudo-Isidorian, had their origin among the Franks, and showed the aims and the needs of the Frankish reformers. They set forth three great objects—" freedom from the secular power, establishment of the ecclesiastical hierarchy with a firm discipline, and centralisation of organisation upon which all could depend."[1] They represented, in fact, a scheme of reform and the way in which a somewhat unscrupulous reformer imagined it could best be carried out. Probably the forged decretals were concocted at Rheims, or possibly at Mainz, and they were first used in a critical case in 866, when a bishop of Soissons, deposed by Hincmar, Archbishop of Rheims, appealed to the pope on the ground that the power of deposition by the decretals belonged to him alone. It is difficult

[1] Dr. C. L. Wells, *The Age of Charlemagne*, p. 434.

to believe that when Nicolas I. accepted them he was not aware that they were not the genuine writings of the popes whose work they professed to be : he can hardly have thought that Spain (where it was said that they had been discovered) was more likely to have kept papal documents safely than the Roman Chancery itself. Their importance was, however, not evident at first. In the ninth and tenth centuries comparatively little was made of them. It was in the eleventh and the centuries which followed that a gigantic edifice of papal assumption was to be built upon them by popes who were fired with a true zeal to reform the world, and who, not doubting their authenticity, found in them an instrument ready to their hands.

The weakness of the papacy in the tenth century was indeed such that no theory could give it respect in Europe. The weakness of the Church was heralded by that of the Empire. The Carling house expired in **The decay** contempt almost as great as that which had **of the** fallen on the Merwings. In Gaul the **papacy.** Norman had won fair provinces on the coast; and the house of the Counts of Paris came in the tenth century to rule over the Franks. There the Church remained strong as the State decayed, and it was the great archbishopric of Rheims which gave the crown to the line of Hugh the Great. In Germany the dynasty of the Carlings became extinct. In Rome the power over the city fell into the hands of the local nobility; and the period was made infamous by the lives of Theodora and Marozia, who were the paramours of popes. The tale of the age of disgrace which marks the greater part of the tenth century is of no importance in the history of the Church. A succession of popes, whom their contemporaries certainly did not believe to be infallible, followed each other in rapid procession. John X. alone (914–28) has any claim to greatness; but he, like the others, was deeply stained with the vices, political if not moral, of his age. It was not until the Saxon Otto came to Italy like a knight-errant to redress the wrongs of the Northern princes, and was crowned at Rome in 962, that the Church in Italy began to revive from its ashes. He deposed and set up popes; and he gave to the papacy something of the bracing ideals which the new life of Gaul and Germany inspired.

The moral weakness of the papacy, the political weakness of Italy, had founded the Empire anew, as it had been founded anew in 800. The revival of the Empire under Charles the Great, and again under Otto, was not due to political considerations only; it was due also to the force of religious ideas.

One great characteristic of the revived Empire in German hands was the important part played in its policy by missions, and, it must be added, missionary wars. It was said of Charles the Great by his eulogists that he converted Saxons and Vandals and Frisians by the Word and the sword: and this thought was embodied in a series of wars which have been somewhat fancifully compared to the Crusades of later days. Otto I. thrice invaded the land of the Slavs and made all the barbarians from the Oder to the Elbe admit his lordship. Six new bishoprics were founded as his sway spread, and the bishop of Magdeburg was raised to be " archbishop and metropolitan of the whole race of the Slavs beyond the Elbe which has

The religious revival of the Empire under the Saxons.

been, or still remains to be, converted to God." But though it was a real work of civilisation, a work which made for peace, that the German Cæsars undertook, it was not a Crusade. A Crusade was a war to win back from the infidel what had once been the patrimony of the Crucified: the wars of the Ottos were directed to extend their own sway, and, as ever, the true work of the converting Church was not helped but hindered by the arms and enterprises of soldiers and statesmen. When the tribes revolted against the government of the Germans, they often disowned their Christianity and destroyed their churches. Under Otto III. the Empire did not recover what she had lost, and the province of Magdeburg remained for nearly half its extent in heathen hands. The Church suffered from this association. Where the mission of S. Boniface had been purely spiritual, the work of his successors was often hampered by the ambition of the emperors. In the lands alike of Eastern and Western Franks the Church was often led to lean on the State, and the results, of slackness, corruption, weakness, were inevitable. The rich endowments which were poured upon the Church were not always wisely given or wisely used. The Cæsars themselves showered gifts: Otto the Great surpassed all his predecessors in lavishness,[1] and his dynasty followed in his steps. But the honours and riches were given quite as much for political as for religious objects. In the bishops and abbats the sovereigns found the wisest servants, the most capable administrators. As among the West Franks under the

Otto the Great's endowments in Germany.

---

[1] See H. A. L. Fisher, *The Medieval Empire*, ii. p. 65; Hauck, *Kirchengeschichte Deutschlands*, iii. 57–9.

Merwings, so now among the East Franks, the great ecclesiastics were the supports of the monarchy, the real governors of the country. It was thus that they came to owe their position—if not their election always yet certainly their confirmation—to the imperial will. As in Rome the emperors were stretching forth a hand to control the elections to the papacy, so in Germany there was growing up at the end of the tenth century the practice of imperial control over the things of the Church. The policy of the Ottos and the reformation of the papacy were certain ultimately to lead to the contest concerning investitures. High clerical office had come too often to be bought and sold, and the churches were becoming mere appanages of the great princi-palities. It was wise of Otto I. to try to win from the dukes the power they had obtained : but it was not for the good of the Church that the power should be even in the imperial hands.

Otto I. died in 973. He had begun the reformation of the papacy. His son and grandson succeeded him, Otto II. in 973, Otto III. in 983. In 996 **Otto III.** died Pope John XV., a Roman whom the **and the** Frankish chronicler, Abbo of Fleury, declares **popes.** to have been lustful of filthy lucre and venal in all his acts. To Otto the clergy, senate, and people of Rome submitted the election of his successor. He chose his own cousin Bruno, "a man of holiness, of wisdom, and of virtue,"—news, to quote the same saintly writer, more precious than gold and precious stones. His throne was insecure : the Roman noble Crescentius drove him from it, but he won his way back and over-came one who had been set up as an anti-pope. He died in 999.

At the close of the tenth century a pope and an emperor of great ideas stand forth from the blackness of an age when, according to the evidence of councils and of monastic chronicles alike, vice was rampant— "the more powerful oppress the weaker, and men are like fishes in the sea, which everywhere in turn devour one another"—and the bishops and clergy alike neglected their duties. Otto III. (983–1002), the offspring of the German who sat on the imperial throne and the daughter of the Cæsars of the East, made himself a real ruler of the Empire in Church as well as in State, and after the disputed succession of his cousin Bruno (Gregory V., 996–99) placed on the papal throne the first of the great line of later medieval popes. Gregory V. was the first pope of transalpine birth imposed by the Germans; Gerbert was the first of the French popes. It needed the imperial army to keep Gregory on the throne, and to crush the last of the Roman princelets who had made the papacy infamous; Gerbert (Silvester II., 999–1003) was only able to remain in the

Gerbert. eternal city so long as Otto was there to protect him. But Gerbert's greatness belonged to a sphere far wider than that of the local papacy. He was a scholar in the ancient classics, a logician, mathematician, astronomer and musician, a great collector of books and a great teacher of men. An Aquitanian by birth, he was brought up at Aurillac, and then passed from one place of study to another, till, by the influence of the Emperor Otto I., he settled at Rheims in 972. His school was a famous one: among those whom he taught were many bishops, Robert the future king of the Franks and Otto the future emperor. From Rheims he went as abbat to

Bobbio, where the necessary severity of his rule provoked such opposition that he was obliged to return to Gaul. He returned in time to win the influence of the great see of Rheims on behalf of the child heir of Otto II., who died at the end of 983, and to take part in the diplomacy which ended in the transfer of the West Frankish crown to Hugh the duke of the Franks. When Arnulf, of the very Karling house which had been dispossessed, became archbishop, and tried to hand over Rheims to his kindred, Gerbert, the steadfast supporter of the "Capetians," was made his successor. The election was of more than doubtful legality, and the politics, papal and imperial, of the time still further complicated the question : it was only settled by the transference of Gerbert, on the nomination of his old pupil, Otto III., to the see of Ravenna. From 998 he remained in Italy till his death. In 999 he became pope, and then he gave himself, heart and soul, to forward

In Gaul

and in Italy.

the great schemes, missionary, reforming, imperial, which were indeed as much his own as those of the enthusiastic genius of the young emperor. The old offices of the " republic " were revived and harmonised, as in the East, with the Christian character of the imperial power. Pope and emperor worked hand in hand for the conversion of the barbarians : it is said that it was Silvester who gave the kingship to the Hungarian Duke Stephen, as a son of the Christian Empire and the holy see of the imperial city. In the unquiet days of his papacy he was yet able to set an example of wisdom, counsel, godliness, charity, which formed an epoch in the regeneration of the Roman episcopate. Zealous, loyal, inspired by an overpowering sense of duty,

Silvester II. in a short time fulfilled a long time and **Pope Silvester II.** left a mark on the history of the Middle Ages such as was made by but few even of its greatest men. At his death in 1003 the age of reform had started on its way; and his was the light which had directed its beginnings. Thus in the West the end of the period shows the Empire and the papacy of one mind, eager for a spiritual reform in the Church, for Christian and missionary ideals in the State, not careful to delimit the provinces of Church and State, but eager rather for unity of action as well as sentiment in the cause of Christian extension and endeavour.

Though the contest was not yet over, it might be said with confidence that the Church of Christ had won over the barbarians. Missionaries and martyrs had changed the face of Europe, and the fierce tribes which were pouring over the Continent in the fifth **The end of the Dark Age.** century, barbarous and heathen, were now for the most part tamed and converted to the love of Christ. Out of a land which had been wild and barbarous, and where one of the greatest of saints and missionaries had met his death, had come a revival in Christian form of the old imperial idea, and the great men who had been nourished by it had given new health to the central Church of Europe. For the moment, the Empire and the Papacy, Germany and the new temporal State in the hands of the Roman bishop, were united to lead the Christian nations and to convert the heathen on their borders. In the East remained the magnificent fabric of the immemorial Empire, active still in missionary labour and setting an example of the union of Church and State in agreement to which the West could never attain. The eleventh century was to bring to East and West alike, with new responsibilities, new difficulties in action and new problems in thought. Everywhere it was for unity men strove, the unity which if in its main aspect it was political, was on its spiritual and ideal side embodied in the visible Church of Christ.

APPENDIX I

LIST OF EMPERORS AND POPES, 461–1003

POPES.	EMPERORS.	
	WEST.	EAST.
		457 Leo I.
461 Hilarus	461 Severus	
	467 Anthemius	
468 Simplicius		
	472 Olybrius	
	473 Glycerius	
	474 Julius Nepos	474 Zeno
	475 Romulus Augus-tulus	
483 Felix III.		
		491 Anastasius I.
492 Gelasius I.		
496 Anastasius II.		
498 Symmachus		
514 Hormisdas		
		518 Justin I.
523 John I.		
526 Felix IV.		
		527 Justinian I.
530 Boniface II.		
532 John II.		
535 Agapetus I.		
536 Silverius		
537 Vigilius		
555 Pelagius I.		
560 John III.		
		565 Justin II.
574 Benedict I.		
578 Pelagius II.		
		578 Tiberius II.
		582 Maurice

POPES.	EMPERORS.	
	WEST.	EAST.
590 Gregory I.		
		602 Phocas
604 Sabinianus		
607 Boniface III.		
607 Boniface IV.		
		610 Heraclius
615 Deusdedit		
618 Boniface V.		
625 Honorius I.		
638 Severinus.		
640 John IV.		
		641 { Heracleonas / Constantine III.
642 Theodorus I.		642 Constans II.
649 Martin I.		
654 Eugenius I.		
657 Vitalianus.		
		668 Constantine IV.
672 Adeodatus		
676 Domnus I.		
678 Agatho		
682 Leo II.		
683 Benedict II.		
685 John V.		685 Justinian II.
687 Sergius I.		
		694 Leontius
		697 Tiberius III.
701 John VI.		
705 John VII.		705 Justinian II. (restored)
708 Sisinnius		
708 Constantine		
		711 Philippicus
		713 Anastasius II.
715 Gregory II.		715 Theodosius III.
		717 Leo III.
731 Gregory III.		
741 Zacharias		741 Constantine V.
752 Stephen II.		
752 Stephen III.		
757 Paul I.		
768 Stephen III. (or IV.)		
772 Hadrian I.		
		775 Leo IV.
		779 Constantine VI.
795 Leo III.		
		797 Irene

POPES.	EMPERORS.	
	WEST.	EAST.
	800 Charles I.	
		802 Nicephorus I.
		811 Stauracius
		811 Michael I.
		813 Leo V.
	814 Louis I.	
816 Stephen IV.		
817 Paschal I.		
		820 Michael II.
824 Eugenius II.		
827 Valentinus		
827 Gregory IV.		
		829 Theophilus
	840 Lothar I.	
		842 Michael III.
844 Sergius II.		
847 Leo IV.		
855 Benedict III.	855 Louis II.	
	(in Italy)	
858 Nicolas I.		
867 Hadrian II.		867 Basil I.
872 John VIII.		
	875 Charles II.	
	(West Franks)	
882 Marinus I.	882 Charles III.	
	(East Franks)	
884 Hadrian III.		
885 Stephen V.		
		886 Leo VI.
891 Formosus	891 Guido (in Italy)	
	894 Lambert	
	(in Italy)	
896 Boniface VI.	896 Arnulf	
896 Stephen VI.	(East Franks)	
897 Romanus		
897 Theodorus II.		
898 John IX.		
900 Benedict IV.		
	901 Louis III.	
	(in Italy)	
903 Leo V.		
903 Christopher		
904 Sergius III.		
911 Anastasius III.		
		912 Constantine VII.
		(till 958)

POPES.	EMPERORS.	
	WEST.	EAST.

POPES.	WEST.	EAST.	
913 Lando		912 Alexander	Co-Emperors
914 John X.		919 Romanus I.	
	915 Berengar (in Italy)	944 { Constantine VIII Stephanus	
928 Leo VI.			
929 Stephen VII.			
931 John XI.	———		
936 Leo VII.			
939 Stephen VIII.			
942 Marinus II.			
946 Agapetus II.			
955 John XII.			
		958 Romanus II.	
	962 Otto I.		
963 Leo VIII.		963 Basil II.	Co-Emperors
[964 Benedict V.]		963 Nicephorus II.	
965 John XIII.			
973 Benedict VI.	973 Otto II.	969 John I.	
974 Domnus II.		976 Constantine IX.	
974 Benedict VII.			
983 John XIV.	983 Otto III.		
985 John XV.			
996 Gregory V.			
999 Silvester II.			
	1002 Henry (II.)		
1003 John XVII.			

NOTE.—This list is for the most part that adopted by Dr. Bryce, *Holy Roman Empire;* but the dates might be slightly varied by reference to Duchesne, K. Müller, and Funk (Weltzer and Welte, *Kirchenlexicon*). It may also be noted that the popes were frequently not elected till the year after the death of their predecessors.

APPENDIX II

A SHORT BIBLIOGRAPHY

I. A list of original authorities for the whole of the period 461–1003 would be too long in proportion to the text of this book, but a few of the most important may be mentioned for the sake of those who wish to begin to study the period at first hand. Any such study should include :—

Evagrius, ed. Bidez and Parmentier, 1898.
Zachariah of Mitylene [translation], ed. Hamilton and Brooks, 1899.
Bede, ed. Ch. Plummer, 1895.
Procopius, ed. Haury (in course of publication).
Joannes Diaconus, *Vita S. Gregorii*, ed. Migne, and *Zeitschrift für Katholische Theologie*, XI., 158–73.
Gregory the Great, *Letters*, ed. Ewald and Hartmann, 1887, etc.
Paulus Diaconus, ed. Waitz, 1878.
Monumenta Moguntina, ed. Jaffé, 1866.
Gregory of Tours, ed. Arndt and Krusch, 1884–5.
Liber Pontificalis, ed. Duchesne, 1886–92.
Liudprand, ed. Dümmler, 1877.
Letters of Gerbert, ed. Havet, 1889.
Regesta Pontificum Romanorum, ed. Jaffé, 1851, 2nd ed. 1885.
Mansi, *Concilia*, 1759–98.
Einhard, *Vita Caroli Magni*, ed. Pertz and Waitz, 1880.

II. Reference to the other authorities can be most easily found through modern works, from which the following is a selection :—

Milman, *History of Latin Christianity.*
Gibbon, *Decline and Fall of the Roman Empire* (ed. Bury).

Bury, *History of the Later Roman Empire*.

Bryce, *Holy Roman Empire*.

Oman, *The Dark Ages*.

Hodgkin, *Italy and her Invaders*.

Hauck, *Kirchengeschichte Deutschlands*.

Harnack, *Dogmengeschichte*.

Duchesne, *Les Églises Separées*.

    „   *Les Premiers Temps de L'État Pontifical*.

H. Leclercq, *L'Afrique chrétienne*.

    „   *L'Espagne chrétienne*.

M. J. Labourt, *Le Christianisme dans l'Empire perse*.

P. J. Pargoire, *L'Église byzantine, de 527 à 847*.

A. J. Butler, *The Arab Conquest of Egypt*.

Diehl, *L'Afrique byzantine*.

    „   *Justinien*.

    „   *Études sur l'administration byzantine dans l'Exarchat de Ravenne*.

F. H. Dudden, *Gregory the Great*.

Hefele, *History of the Councils*.

Gasquet, *L'Empire byzantin et la Monarchie franque*.

Hutton, *The Church of the Sixth Century*.

Besse, *S. Wandrille*.

Du Bourg, *S. Odon*.

Martin, *S. Colomban*.

Hodgkin, *Charles the Great*.

Davis, *Charlemagne*.

Fisher, *The Medieval Empire*.

Hunt, *The English Church, 597–1066*.

Margoliouth, *Mohammed*.

Gardner, *Theodore of Studium*.

Marin, *De Studio Constantinopolitano*.

Lavisse (ed.), *Histoire de France*.

Marignan, *Études sur la civilisation française (la société mérovingienne)*.

Lützow, *Bohemia*.

Morfill, *Poland*.

Rambaud, *Histoire de la Russie*.

Poole, *Illustrations of Medieval Thought*.

Kraus, *Geschichte der Christlichen Kunst*, I.

Potthast, *Bibliotheca Medii Ævi*.

INDEX

Belisarius, 30, 61, 105
Benedict Biscop, 115, 169
Benedict of Nursia, S., 34-9, 53, 58, 163 ; his Rule, 35-7, 58-9, 69, 119, 121, 171, 173, 175 ; the Benedictines, 35-8, 60, 62, 137
Bercta, Kentish queen, 186
Berno, abbat of Cluny, 173-4
Besançon, 56, 173
Béziers, 146
Bishops, their position under Justinian, 24-5 ; share in the civil government of Italy, 33-4 ; without dioceses in the Celtic Church, 114 ; "Universal Bishop," 66, 175 ; bless the people at the Eucharist, 190
Blemmyes, Ethiopic tribe, converted, 111
Bobbio, 53, 56, 201
Boethius, 32
Bohemia, Christianity in, 127-9 ; Bohemian princess brings about the conversion of Poland, 125
Boïar, title of Bulgarian magnates, 124
Boleslav I., duke of Bohemia, brother of S. Wenceslas (died 967), 128
Boleslav II., "the Pious," duke of Bohemia (967-99), 128, 129
Boniface, S. (Winfrith), 130, 136-40, 142, 147, 198
Boris, Bulgarian king, 124
Bořivoj, Bohemian duke, baptized, 128
Boso, bishop of Merseburg, 126
Braga, councils at (563, 572), 74
Bremen, archbishopric, 130, 142
Bretislav II., king of Bohemia (1092-1100), 127
Britain, 83, 88 ; Christianity in, 113 ff. ; early British Church, 183 ; ritual in the British Church, 183. See England
Brittany, 115
Brunichild, 43, 48-9, 56, 74-5, 171
Bruno (Pope Gregory V.), cousin of Otto III., 199, 200

Bruno, missionary to the Prussians, 125
Brythons, Celts of Britain, their Church, 113, 183
Bulgarians, a Finnish race, conversion of, 124 ; they and their Church, 13, 23, 44, 84, 128, 193
Burgundians, 41 ; Frankish kings of, 49, 55-6, 135
Bury, Dr. J. B., quoted, 21 n., 46-7, 113
Byzacene, African see, 106
Byzantine architecture, 25-8, 100, 106 ; Church and Patriarchate, 91, and see Constantinople ; Empire, see Empire, Eastern

Cælian Hill at Rome, 60, 64
Cæsarius, bishop of Arles, 72, 81
Calabria, 157, 162
Candace, title of the queens of Abyssinia, 111
Canons, collection of, 85 ; canon law, 194-5 ; canon of the Mass, 181-2, 190
Canterbury, 115, 185-6
Capetians, House of Hugh the Great, duke of the Franks, 201
Carisiacum (Quierzy), 151
Carling House. See Karlings
Carloman, son of Charles Martel, brother of Pippin the Short, 144-5, 147, 149
Carloman, son of Pippin the Short, brother of Charles the Great, 148, 150-1
Carthage, taken by the Vandals, 103 ; by the Muhammadans, 77, 109 ; Church of, survival, 110 ; bishop of, 67, 103-6, 108
Cassiodorus, 30, 38
Catholicos, primate of the Monophysite Armenian Church, 84, 95 ; of the "Church of the East," 96 ; of the Persian Church, 93-4, 99
Celibacy of the clergy. See Marriage
Celtic Church, 113-17, and see Ireland ; Celtic Easter, 55, 114 ;